"Pastor Pete Fiske is an extraordinary man who lives an ordinary life. It is this trait that shapes him as a human being. His love for those who are downtrodden and hurt is what magnifies his soul for others to see within. Pete's accomplishments are nothing less than miracles from the Lord. It is an honor to call him a friend. Pete touches all with love, humility and honesty. He is indeed a real gem."

- Patricia Marshall MS, LADC, Author of *Trading Faces*

DON'T BURN MY HOUSE DOWN

PETER H. FISKE

Copyright © 2025 by Peter Hadley Fiske. All rights reserved. No part of this book may be used or reproduced in any manner without written permission except in the case of brief quotations when properly cited.

For You Lord and Your goodness. My life started when You decided that I would exist. You have taken care of me all my life. You have guided my steps, given me direction and purpose. You were with me in the dark of the night and You led me through the fire. You have protected me from my enemies. You even prepared a banquet table in the presence of my enemy. You commissioned me to work with criminals during incarceration and after release. You gave me love for people the world discards and locks away. You have kept all your promises. You cleaned up my mistakes and messes. You are with me in whatever I do and wherever I go, as You promised. I have lived in Your goodness and will continue into eternity.

Thank You Lord for my parents Robert and Louise, for my three younger sisters Robin, Becky and Mickey, for the wife of my youth Agnes and our four sons Chris, Lee, Adam and Nate, and for the wife of my senior years Joanne and our son Sal.

"If we share the Gospel with all our hearts, even the roots of the trees will tremble wherever we walk."

Rev. Agnes Fiske

This is the story of my journey into prison ministry as a guide to hearing and following God's calling. God is an opportunist and accepted the offer of my life in service to His Kingdom. But He wrote the job description, not me. I believe He planned my life and purpose long, long ago. My life began when my true Father decided that I would exist.

> "He chose us in Him before the foundation of the world, that we should be holy and without blame before Him in love."
>
> *Eph 1:4*

Table of Contents

Acknowledgements xvii
Preface xix
Introduction xxii

I. EARLY DAYS

The Beginning 27
Lost 31
Trinity Episcopal Church 33
Blind Date: What Mother Did Not Know about Peter 38

II. THE CALL TO MINISTRY

Lost & Born Again 47
The Shooting Star 51
A Vision for Evangelism & The Plan for Bringing
 Our Community to Christ 53
Leaving The Episcopal Church 57
Morrisville 58
The Trip 65
Marriage Encounter & Cursillo 72
Chronos Vs. Kairos 74
Dream: January 10, 1990 76
Peace 80

It All Comes Together, 1991   83
United Christian Assembly   86
Prophecy: 3-1-92 by Pastor Duane Hodgeman   88
Prophecy for Pete and Agnes Fiske   90
Agnes at United Christian Assembly – April, 1992   91
The Walk Home   92

III.   GROWING IN FAITH

The Contractor   97
Sell Your House   102
Burn My House Down   106
Kairos   108
Church Service   110
A Walk in the Dark   113
The House Sale   117
Christmas, 1993   119
Happy New Year, 1994   121
Panic & Repent   123
The Rose by Agnes Fiske   125
The Snow Geese   127
The Master   129
The Car   132
Sweet Perfume   135
The Kirby Man   137
End of a Chapter: The Death of Agnes   139
The Funeral   145
A New Chapter Begins: The Hand   147
Hello Joanne Falise by Joanne "Jo" Fiske   149
The River of Life to Jesus Vs. The Downward Landslide
        into The Abyss   152
The Vacuum Cleaner   154
Spring Is Here and So Is The Upper Room
        by Joanne "Jo" Fiske   156
Isaiah Vision 40   158

IV. LESSONS FROM THE FOREST

God Speaks   163
Life is Like a Forest   165
The Pathway (Coyotes I)   168
The Short Leash   171
The Little Dog   173
Twilight and Short Leash II   176
Dawn   179
Embedded Roots   180
Wildfires   182
Benched   185
Blink (Coyotes II)   187
The Risen Son is Rising over Vermont!   188
The Foundation   189
Bloom in Your Garden!   191
The Darkness   193
Morning   195
Joshua 1:9   196
Focus on God   197
Three Trees   199
In The Valley   200

V. CHURCH AT PRISON: STORIES BY AND ABOUT INMATES

Church At Prison Poem   203
Patmos Christian College   205
Sean Allain's Story   208
The Release   211
Letter to Bob Sawyer from Agnes Fiske   213
Inside, On The Way Outside – James Rivers   216
Life Inside Prison for a Christian Inmate
    by Bob Sawyer   220

Fleabag by Fleabag
    (with help from Norman, Birger, and Pastor Pete)   222
The Death of Fleabag by Bob Sawyer   225
Paying Homage to the "Ramen Empire"
    by J. Lee Mackenzie   226
The Book "Bible" by Moses Cirrilo   233
Close Custody Deliverance by Rich Gardner   235
Kairos #11 Testimony by Glen   236
Witnessing by Bob Sawyer   237
Renewal of Love after 34 Years by Ramon Valentin   239
Restitution, Inc. by Betsy Wolfenden   241
Odds and Ends by Bob Sawyer   243
Being a Father in Jail by Bob Sawyer   246
Testimony of Pastor Fred Little   248
Rafael's Story: "Historia de la Vida en el Mar"
    by Rafael Mercedes Senereno   251
Choices by Fernand Forcier   253

VI.   MEMORIALS, FUNERALS & REMEMBRANCES

Marian by Fred Little   257
Letter from an Offender's Wife by Emma Duncan   259
Emma Duncan   261
Bill Verrinder - Obituary   262
Bill Verrinder Memorial   263
James Hemingway – Obituary by Sharon Andis   266
Remembering Jimmy by Fred Little   269
Reaching Beyond by Fred Little   271
Phyllis Russell   276

VII.   VERMONT DEPT. OF CORRECTIONS

CSOM (Center for Sex Offender Management)   281
Relations With Vermont Dept. of Corrections
    RE: Wayne Delisle   283

Relocating 1: Wayne Delisle   285
Relocating 2: Tim Szad   287
Letters of Acknowledgement and Gratitude from VT Dept of
    Corrections   290
Agency of Human Services:
    Dept of Corrections, Waterbury   291
Agency of Human Services:
    Dept of Corrections, Probation & Parole, Burlington   292
Vermont Center for Prevention and Treatment
    of Sexual Abuse, Robert J. McGrath   293
Vermont Center for Prevention and Treatment
    of Sexual Abuse, Georgia Cumming   295
Agency of Human Services,
    Northwest State Correctional Facility, Brian M. Bilodeau   297

Acknowledgements

I could not have written this book without the spiritual and loving guidance from, first of all, the Lord Jesus; second, my incredible wife of 39 years, Rev. Agnes Julia Fiske; my editor Salvatore Folisi; a few other authors named herein; and my beloved ministry partner and wife since 2006, Rev. Joanne "Jo" Reed Fiske.

Preface

This collection of stories is offered as a guidebook for others to hear and follow God's calling. In my case it was prison ministry, which was out of the box of my imagination. The mother of a young inmate we were counseling once told us, "I used to drive by that prison daily to work and I always thought to myself, *Ugh, filthy evil people are housed there*, and shiver in disgust and fear. Little did I know my own son would be arrested and live there for several years. I began to go to the visiting room at that same prison to see my son and got to know other men incarcerated there. That was when my heart changed—knowledge can do that—because most of the men I met were nice, polite, regular people like me. Wow, what a difference! It rocked my world and changed my heart towards prisoners and prisons."

Prison ministry?

God placed me where He wanted me—not where I thought I should go to do His work, but where He knew I belonged. Which is something I would have never discovered without His guidance. If you open your heart and trust Him to show you the way, I believe He will guide you to your true path as well.

The purpose of this book is to share my story and provide encouragement to you men and women who are, and will be, called by God into harvest fields that may not yet be defined. You will be anointed with grace, God's unmerited favor, to do what God has chosen you for, whether you feel ready for it or not. Let's just say, He will make it plain, so follow His lead. He has the plan prepared for you!

> "For we are God's masterpiece. He has created us anew in Christ Jesus, so we can do the good things he planned for us long ago."
>
> *Eph 2:10*

> "Your eyes saw my substance, being yet unformed. And in Your book, they all were written, The days fashioned for me, When as yet there were none of them."

Psalm 139:16

God will carry out His purpose through you, provide for you, protect you, anoint you and give you the ability to do and face what is needed.

> "I, the Lord, have called You in righteousness, and will hold Your hand; I will keep You and give You as a covenant to the people, As a light to the Gentiles."

Isaiah 42:6

You may be called to do new things for which there is no textbook, college class or mentor to guide your every step.

> "Thy Word is a lamp unto my feet and a light unto my path."

Psalm 119:105

All you have to do is remember to:

> "Trust in the Lord with all your heart And lean not on your own understanding; In all your ways acknowledge Him, And He shall direct your paths."

Proverbs 3:5-6

The journey starts now!

"It was by faith that Abraham obeyed when God called him to leave home and go to another land that God would give him as his inheritance. He went without knowing where he was going.

Heb 11:8

Only He knows the outcome of what you do and how it ends. He will give you the grace to do and face what is needed.

"He chose us in Him before the foundation of the world, that we should be holy and without blame before Him in love."

Eph 1:4

Introduction

I am not a Biblical Scholar nor a Seminary graduate. I barely graduated from Rutland High School. I failed my senior year, but thanks to my French II teacher, Francis Robillard, who gave me an A on the final exam (I had failed), I was able to graduate in 1962 at the bottom of my class.

I did well in French I, but in French II we sat in enclosed cubicles instead of desks in an open room. We wore headphones while Mr. Robillard spoke into a microphone. That whole scenario put me to sleep in ten minutes!

To this day, sitting while not mentally engaged puts me to sleep. One time in study hall I fell asleep and was rudely awoken by the teacher yelling MR. FISKE! I opened my eyes to discover I had slid out of my desk onto the floor, and the teacher was standing over me looking down.

How utterly embarrassing!

My narcoleptic tendencies were so strong I was nicknamed "Sleepy" in the 1962 Rutland High School Yearbook.

Someday I will go to my first Class of '62 Reunion—but it might be the 62nd reunion for the Class of '62.

Through the keen insight and efforts of my Art teacher, Lucy Doane, who discovered I could draw lines well, I was considered a good candidate to become a draftsman. Of course, it helped that my mother and Lucy were friends and fellow artists. With help from Mr. Canary, my guidance counselor, I was accepted at Vermont Technical College in the Mechanical Engineering Design program. (I learned not to give up, because God works in mysterious ways, though I did not understand it yet.)

Mr. Canary was also my instructor for Driver's Ed. My father didn't let me get my driver's license until the year I turned 18. What a nightmare it was using the clutch for the first time! I had to learn to stop on a hill. Shift with my right hand. Duck foot the gas and clutch at the same time. Roll down the window and stick my arm out to signal turning left, right or stopping. Do all this on a hill, using a clutch, where I had to stop and start and turn all at the same time?

Are you kidding me!

I learned to avoid hills altogether, to stay out of city traffic and drive on back roads like Dad did. Otherwise, I feared getting killed in a horrible accident or having a heart attack the first day of driving!

At the end of the first session, to my surprise, I was still alive. I needed my license because there was this cute girl in Middlebury that I had met and didn't want to rely on Greyhound bus schedules to see her. Even with my acceptance into Technical College, I had to go back to high school for a post-graduate year to take extra math and science courses. More physics, geometry, and trigonometry. I even tried to take Algebra III, but the teacher, Edmund T. Boyce, wouldn't let me in the door of his classroom. I had done well with Algebra I, but had failed Algebra II and had to take it a second time, only to pass with a D. My downfall was logarithms, which my brain couldn't fathom, and, so lieu of understanding, preferred sleep.

To this day I don't understand logarithms or see the need for them. In fact, I avoid them. I will cross the street to avoid one if I see it coming. Ugh! One of a class of auxiliary numbers, to abridge arithmetical calculations, by the use of addition and subtraction in place of multiplication and division. Got that?

Life as a post-graduate high school student was strange. I had a 1949 Pontiac—a "rescue car" my father was going to send to the junk yard. I also had a job working as a stock boy and delivery truck driver for the Boston Market IGA, owned by Mr. Tailbey. Caught between my former childhood but not in college yet, I felt like I was floating between two worlds. Like leaving one shore of Rocky Pond and doggie paddling to the other side. It was a 3-year trip from High School to college graduation.

It was so embarrassing to go to the beach with friends and not know how to swim that one day my good buddy, Allen, and I decided to risk drowning by enacting the world renowned "sink or swim" method. We were at Rocky Pond on top of Pine Hill, a town park with a small beach and a part-time caretaker.

SPLASH!

With the bravery of wartime soldiers we leapt into the water, resolved to swim or die trying. Somehow our arms and legs became coordinated enough to keep us from sinking to the bottom, and we actually swam across the pond and back to the beach on what seemed like a 2 mile journey.

That was victory day!

Upon learning to swim for the very first time we declared ourselves to be expert swimmers. 60-some years later, using the scientific precision of Google Earth, I measured the distance from shore to shore and deduced we had swum maybe a 1/4 mile.

Did the pond shrink in those 65 years?

Or just my imagination?

After that we swam a lot in that spot and had many adventures. One time, late in the afternoon, we were in the middle of Rocky Pond in an old rowboat we had spent hours restoring. But as I pulled too hard on the oars, the sides of the boat fell off. Someone saw the fiasco, left and called the police. Two officers came in a patrol car as it was getting dark to investigate teenagers reportedly vandalizing a whole fleet of boats. What was more surprising was when they made us get out of the pond to question us, we were skinny dipping.

They worked us over using the "good cop / bad cop" technique—one guy yelled at us while the other smiled kindly.

They verified the boat was ours and that it fell apart because it was rotten—so we didn't get charged with a crime. I don't know why we didn't get charged for public nudity. Maybe standing in front of two Rutland Policemen wasn't considered being in public. Or maybe they were amused at our naivety. I guess back in those days the laws weren't so *explicit* on that score.

The bad cop wanted to make us walk the three miles home, but we got a free ride because the good cop was the driver. So it all worked out well for us.

Until I got home ...

Walking in the house my father yelled at me for hanging out with cops. He never asked why I'd gotten a ride home in a patrol car or told me what his issue was. But he was adamant, "Just stay away from cops!" I still remember the good cop who was nice to us. I have had many opportunities in my life as a Prison Pastor to associate with law enforcement and enjoyed it.

And to this day I still avoid skinny dipping and logarithms.

I.

EARLY DAYS

The Beginning

"So the LORD God caused the man to fall into a deep sleep; and while he was sleeping, he took one of the man's ribs and then closed up the place with flesh. Then the LORD God made a woman from the rib he had taken out of the man, and he brought her to the man."

Genesis 2:21-22

Louise Hadley grew up in Rutland, VT. She graduated from Rutland High School in 1933 and became an artist studying under Norman Rockwell and other local art teachers. She was one of the founders and Secretary of the Mid-Vermont Artists Association.

In 1942 the country was engaged in WWII. Louise was 27 and working at the Red Cross, when she met Robert Fiske, a handsome 30 year old farm boy from Weybridge, VT. Robert had come to Rutland to enlist in the military, but had some difficulty with the medical exam. Eventually, he was accepted into the Marines—better known as the "Sea Going Bell Hops" by soldiers in other military branches who made fun of their "pretty" uniforms.

When they met, Louise was pen pals with Vermont soldiers overseas and, as she explained it to me, was engaged to 13 of them at the same time.

Louise was living with her Aunt May Gonyea, a widow in Rutland. After Louise's mother Jesse Gonyea died in 1922, she was raised by Jesse's brother Frank and his wife May. Frank died in 1941 and Louise continued living with May until she met Robert.

Aunt May apparently did not like Robert and was upset that Louise was in love with him—probably because he was from a farm family, drank, and had romanced Louise off her feet! Oh, and also because she soon became pregnant. If you can count, add and subtract, I was conceived sometime between Halloween and Thanksgiving. Though I like candy and a good costume, I prefer to think of myself as a Thanksgiving Creation.

However, in those days unwed mothers were disgraced by society, and I'm sure that infuriated Aunt May. Mom told me that the year she graduated from Rutland High School, in 1933, twenty-five girls were not at graduation because they were pregnant.

WOW!

So on Valentines Day, February 14, 1944—before the baby bump began to show—Robert and Louise eloped and were married in Whitehall, NY.

Mom never told me what happened to her 13 other fiancées. I suppose there are 13 more stories that could be told. How many did not survive the war? She also never told me how eloping affected Aunt May. Maybe a secret story? But in May's later years she lived with us in Weybridge until she passed away, and I don't recall her ever mentioning it. But I do remember Dad telling me that each night he would give Aunt May a teaspoon of brandy that would make her more pleasant to be around. Taking a cue from Dad, many years later that same method worked on my mother in law.

On Sunday morning July 30, 1944, at 2:30 a.m. I was born. The doctor had induced labor for my mother who was expected to die from a kidney infection that had gone systemic. As a result, my life was in danger. I also was born with jaundice from the RH factor and received ultra violet light treatment just after birth. Due to this, when exposed to too much sunshine, I'm prone to occasional skin cancer from having being overdosed on the UV light treatment.

My first name had been pre-arranged to be Jonathon (after my father's younger brother who died at age 15), and my middle name Robert (after my father). If I had come out as a girl, I don't know what the name would have been, but six years later they named my sister Roberta (after my father), and her middle name Louise (after my mother).

My mother did not die as expected. Rather, the nurse came into the room holding me and said, "Louise, you are still with us. What is your son's name?" Without thinking she blurted out "Peter Hadley Fiske." She was envisioning the Apostle Peter and had inserted Hadley, her maiden name, as my middle name.

My father was enrolled in Marine boot camp at Paris Island, NC and unable to protest her spontaneous change of mind. In fact, he did not see me until I was 7 months old, when he was released on leave to attend the funeral of his mother, Mabel Ryder Fiske. After that, he returned to the Marines to train for the planned invasion of Japan.

It could be that my father did not know I existed or what gender I was until he received a letter from my mother. Did they have air mail in 1944? Were they still using Pony Express? Today I can send a letter by Express Mail, email, or instant messaging on social media.

No ponies involved.

❖

After leaving the hospital in Burlington, Louise went to the Homesite Farm in Cornwall, VT where my father's brother Herman Fiske was living with his wife Jane and daughter Linda. Jane was expecting their second child, gender unknown, just as it had been from the day of Adam and Eve's children. If it was going to be a boy, Herman and Jane were going to name him Stephen. If it was a girl, they would call her Judy. As it turned out, Judy came first and Stephen followed a couple of years later. In both cases, it was the nurse and doctor who knew the gender first. The father found out later while he was waiting in the hospital waiting room—where fathers would go when ordered to "Get out of the way and go wait!" because watching the birth was forbidden for fathers.

Usually the father was obedient as he was raised in the days when you did what you were told. Sometimes the hospital shift change came during delivery, and as soon as the baby came out the nurse would tell the new shift nurse, "Take the baby to the father in the waiting room." But during the 40s a lot of fathers were soldiers in the war and not home. And sometimes, when the message to notify the father got lost in the shuffle the nurse assumed there was no father in the waiting room, and the poor guy would be *waiting* and *waiting* and *waiting* until the next day. Sometimes he went home to milk the cows and fell asleep in the barn. It could be a couple of days before somebody was able to remember to find him and tell him that he had a daughter.

Today cell phones make everything more convenient, and the nurse can call the father without knowing where in the world he is and give him the good news. And now with social media on his cell phone, he can see nearly instantaneous photos of the mother and baby, or even livestream of the birth!

Of course, times have changed enormously since the 40s and now fathers are invited to participate in the birthing event first hand.

NO THANK YOU!

If I even see as much as a cow, dog or chipmunk giving birth, I will be sick and faint.

When my son Lee was born the nurse brought him to me in the waiting room and put him in my arms. She opened the blanket and I saw he was a boy, and had ten toes and ten fingers. We worried about those numbers in 1968. We once had a cat with 6 toes on each foot. We worried about these things especially after reading *2 Samuel 21:20*. Yet again, there was war at Gath, where there was a man of great stature who had six fingers on each hand and six toes on each foot, twenty-four in number.

Lee had not been cleaned up from birthing. There was blood and gunk all over him and I struggled to not faint, vomit or run away. I was a good loving father and gently gave him back to the nurse. I did not let that experience keep me from loving him or having more sons.

The next two were "clean as whistles" when I saw them.

Lost

"Therefore, angels are only servants—spirits sent (by God) to care for people who will inherit salvation."

Hebrews 1:14

It was 1947. I was 3 years old and we were living in an old house built at the end of the revolutionary war. My father bought it for about $1,000 after he was released from the Marines. There was no plumbing other than a hand pump on the kitchen sink connected to a cistern in the cellar. My father filled the cistern by draining water from a tank in a truck that came from Middlebury.

There was no electricity. We used kerosene lanterns and a battery operated radio. The ice box kept food cool. The ice man would come with fresh ice periodically. I remember the ice man in Middlebury would leave a pile of ice chips on his tailgate so we kids could have a cold treat in the summer.

We had an outhouse in back of the house. I remember my mother taking me out there at night while carrying a lantern. In cold weather she would sit on the seat to warm it up before putting me on it.

Momma loved me!!

One day I wandered away from home. When my mother realized I was gone, she searched for me frantically, screaming my name amidst choking sobs and tears. I don't know how long I was missing, but she gathered the men in the village to search for me.

We lived a few hundred yards from Otter Creek, which had a small island that split the river into two streams. There was a dam on each stream and two bridges. Some of the men got ropes with grappling hooks and began dragging the river for my body.

My mother watched in horror as the ropes were thrown and pulled through the water again and again. She screamed out to the God she knew: "Please God, my baby, my son ... Where is my boy? Help me please!"

In the midst of her despair, God answered.

Suddenly, amidst the roar of the river pouring over the dam into the rapids below, somehow, she heard a tiny, faint voice coming from way upstream. "Mommy! Mommy!"

She ran uphill to Field Days Road and kept a fierce pace for a quarter mile. She leapt over a cattle fence, ran through the pasture, around trees and brush to the river bank where I was hanging onto a bush at the edge of the deep water. She picked me up and held me, thanking God for saving her little boy. She carried me home with tears of relief and joy streaming down her face. The search team met her in the front yard of our home and cheered.

My mother never mentioned my father in her telling of the story, so he must have been working that day. When he got home that night I can only imagine the dramatic display he must have witnessed.

Trinity Episcopal Church

"For we are God's handiwork, created in Christ Jesus to do good works, which God prepared in advance for us to do."

Eph 2:10 NLT

When I was 10 years old I started going to Trinity Episcopal Church in Rutland with my neighborhood buddy Chucky Oakman. In catechism classes we memorized the Creed and The Lords Prayer, then when we turned 12 we went to Confirmation where Bishop Vedder Van Dyck laid hands on my head and blessed me.

The day before Confirmation, Chuckie, Allen and I hitchhiked to Lake Bomoseen in Castleton to go fishing. For some reason I wore my dress shoes, my backup tennis shoes being PF Flyers. During the fishing trip the sole of one shoe came unstitched, flopping in the air every step I took and making it hard to walk properly.

PANIC!

How could I dress up for Confirmation the next day with a flip-flopping shoe!

Back in Rutland I discovered my PF Flyers were worn and had a hole in one toe. There was no way I could go to Confirmation wearing grubby shoes. Heaven would open up and send a lightning bolt down to evaporate me in front of Bishop Vedder Van Dyk.

To make matters worse, I was already on shaky ground with the Bishop. I had been at Rock Point Episcopal Summer Camp in Burlington that summer, and us kids got a pillow fight going. It extended out of the dorm rooms and into the hallways, downstairs into the dining room and classrooms.

Well, wouldn't you know it, I was at the top of a staircase waiting to ambush Joey. When I heard him coming up the stairs, I let the feather-filled missile fly. But it wasn't Joey; it was the Bishop!

My memory goes blank at that point.

Either the Bishop caught me or I escaped the scene—yes, there's a big difference between the two, but the fact that I can't remember only proves that I was thoroughly traumatized! All this to say I was petrified to show up for Confirmation with grubby PF Flyers or shoes with one sole flopping when I walked. I was one of those kids who couldn't rub my head and pat my stomach at the same time while whistling Dixie, so trying to walk normal in flopping shoes would be impossible.

Needing a miracle, I went downtown to the New York Clothing Store that was owned by our next door neighbor, Mr. Cantor. I asked him if I could get a pair of Buster Brown dress shoes for $8 and charge them. I said my mother would pay him when she got home from work.

Being our neighbor, he knew we were poor and my father was a laborer who frequently came home drunk. He said "No!"

Thinking quick on my feet, I remembered Chuckie and I had the same shoe size, so I went to his house and asked if I could borrow a pair of shoes. In those days people, especially kids, had one pair of dress shoes and one pair of tennis shoes or, as we sometimes called them, sneakers. Chuckie was wearing his dress shoes to Confirmation but also had a new pair of PF Flyers that were nice and clean. He loaned them to me for the special occasion.

The next day the Bishop laid his hands on my head, maybe after I kissed his ring? (Why does that thought occur to me now?) Apparently, he didn't remember me and had forgotten about the pillow ambush that nearly knocked him down the staircase.

With his holy hands on my head, he mumbled or chanted some holy words I didn't understand. What was imparted to me that day was a sense of relief that a lightning bolt never came my way. I had escaped horrible consequences, able to live another day. Cats have nine lives, but how many do I have?

❖

The question of cats reminds me of King Basil, a cat we had back in '56 that was tough outdoors but mild and cuddly inside—a combo Street Monster and House Angel all wrapped into one. Unfortunately, I watched him get hit in front of our house by a car speeding up Grove Street. After the car drove off, I went over and could see he was dead. I picked him up to take him home and he was stiffer than a board. Dead as dead can be. I didn't know what to do with him, so I stuffed him in the garbage can on our back porch. Two days later I heard my mother scream. I ran to the kitchen where she was pointing outside at one of the garbage cans. King Basil was alive and sitting on top of the lid, hungry and meowing. A cat ghost? No, I thought, just one of his nine lives.

❖

Now that Chuckie and I were officially confirmed, we felt like important people in the Episcopal Diocese of Vermont serving as altar boys. Right about that time, Chuckie and I both had a crush on Cindy Throop, the daughter of Parish Priest Fr. Robert Throop. We discussed the fact that we both liked her and could see she was really cute. But we were friends and didn't want to let a girl come between us and wreck our friendship. So we agreed to share her between us. After one of us asked her out, our first date was a Saturday afternoon matinée at the Grand Movie Theater, where Chuckie sat on her left and I sat on her right.
Weird!
(But it was an affordable date because in those days you could get into the theater for 12 cents, easily obtained by trading in a six pack of empty Coke bottles.)

I think Cindy wasn't very impressed with us because neither of us had another date with her. Or maybe her father stepped in after the first date and made a rule that altar boys couldn't date his beautiful daughter. So much for our important positions in the Episcopal Church.

We had originally joined the church children's choir, but after our voices dropped from sopranos to sketchy altos or tenors we got transferred to the altar boy position. I worked for Father John Nourse, a retired mailman who was ordained as a Curate and assistant to the Parish Priest. Father Nourse was a scholar who studied many subjects and had a wonderful encyclopedia-like memory. At the time he was studying Russian as his fourth or fifth language. Father Nourse was also skilled at making the fancy gold threaded ornate vestments he and other priests wore.

Father Nourse was the first adult person in my life who talked to me as if I was an important individual and not a kid. He would treat me to breakfast after an early morning communion service, at which, normally, no one was in attendance other than the two of us.

Every time he saw me, he would point his finger at me and proclaim, "Thou art Peter and upon this rock I shall build My church, and the gates of hell shall not prevail against it" (*Matt 6:18 KJV*).

God used Father Nourse to speak me into the ministry He was preparing me for. As with Father Nourse, this calling was to be after retiring from my secular job.

"He chose us in Him before the foundation of the world."

Eph 1:4a

I was familiar with all the sacramental garments, linens, candles and snuffers, altar tools and hymns. I memorized the words from the Book of Common Prayer for the Eucharist Service in Rite I and eventually Rite II. But I did not personally know Jesus nor much about Him.

"You saw me before I was born. Every day of my life was recorded in your book. Every moment was laid out before a single day had passed."

Psalm 139:16 NLT

I remember winning a plastic cross with Jesus on it at the Rutland County Fair. I hung it on my bedroom wall and can still see it in my mind. That cross was my personal connection with God at that time.

My first memory of praying was in our attic on Grove Street in Rutland when I was in 7th grade at Meldon Jr High School. I was not a good student and asked God to help me complete a homework assignment for class. I couldn't finish it because I had left the text book at school and needed another day. Having not completed the assignment, I had to go to school and confess to the teacher that it was not done. But God heard my prayer! The teacher was out sick the next day and the class was canceled. So He gave me the day I needed, and I avoided being embarrassed and ashamed.

"For I know the plans I have for you," declares the Lord,
"plans to prosper you and not to harm you, plans to give you hope and a future. Then you will call on me and come and pray to me, and I will listen

to you. You will seek me and find me when you seek me with all your heart."

Jeremiah 29:11-13

Blind Date
(What My Mother Did Not Know about Peter)

It was April of 1965. I would be graduating from Vermont Technical College in Randolph Center later that spring and had a job waiting for me at IBM in Essex Junction. My mother was concerned that I didn't have a date for the College Prom in May. My fiancée Pamela had dumped me in the summer of '63 when she realized I was going to college for two years, saying she couldn't wait for me and needed someone with a good paycheck.

UGH! Heartbreak!

Sometime down the road I heard she and her husband opened up a small diner in Bristol, where eventually she stole all the cash from the diner safe and ran away with the cook.

Whew! Close call for me. Thank you Lord!

Being a loving mother, Mom always warned me about the "hot chicks" I brought home: "Where did you find that dame? Don't you know girls like that have diseases?" And my father had warned me about getting involved with Pamela because he knew the family. In this case, they were both right.

Mom was determined to help me make a good choice—for a prom date and, if she had her druthers, for a wife to boot. At that time I lived on campus during the week and would come home on Friday evenings for the weekend. One Saturday, Mom invited me to meet her for lunch at The Rutland Herald Newspaper where she worked as the day editor. When I got to her office, Mom was there with a skinny, puffy-haired girl with whom we were to have lunch at The Kong Chow Chinese Restaurant. Mom said, "This is Agnes Dutelle, she is going to have lunch with us." A strange feeling rose from the pit of my stomach and traveled up to my brain, at which point I probably said, "Hi!" and smiled like a good son should.

Agnes worked with Mom at The Rutland Herald and they had become good friends. Apparently, Agnes had been visiting our home, bringing presents to my little sisters, and was affectionately called "The Good Fairy Agnes." Being at college during the week I had never met Agnes, but had heard about "The Good Fairy Agnes." In my mind she was one of those "Goody Goody Two Shoe" girls that didn't interest me.

At the restaurant we sat at a booth, Mom beside me and Agnes across the table. I think my mind was spinning because I can't remember anything beyond Mom slipping a ten dollar bill under the table into my hand which, believe it or not, was enough to pay for lunch back in those days, and saying, "I have to go back to the office."

HOLY COW!

Panic!!

Obviously, I knew Mom was setting me up with a date for the College Prom, and I just wanted to quietly slide out of the booth onto the floor and melt away. But God had used my mother to launch His plan. I was frozen and couldn't move. It would have been undignified and embarrassing to run away, so I just sat there looking at this skinny, puffy-haired girl who was smiling at me and waiting for me to say something intelligent. After all, I was graduating from Engineering College with passing grades in calculus, physics, analytical trigonometry, pool and poker. What could I say? "What are you going to order?"

Somehow, I survived and ordered Chicken Chow Mien for myself. That was my mother's favorite Chinese dish. Agnes ordered something and started the conversation because I was still in shock and didn't know how to talk with the Good Fairy Agnes. Girls that I had dated were bold hot chicks that approached me first—not like the princess darling sitting across from me courtesy of my mother.

Chinese food was and still is a favorite of mine. As I ate I calmed down and was able to respond with conversation that must have been acceptable because by the end of the meal Agnes was acting happy and seemed more human. She was also very nice to be with.

I learned Agnes was so smart she had graduated high school a year early, in 1963. During her last year of Catholic High School at Mount Saint Joseph she volunteered in the local hospital ER as an intake assistant where she met a patient named George Forrest, who came in with a gunshot wound in his leg. She told me she talked with him and what a nice guy he was.

George had been shot by an Addison County Sheriff during the armed robbery of a gas station. I remembered George from Lake Dunmore where I worked as a dishwasher at a Jewish Boys Summer Camp. He was one of the "Salisbury Bad Assers," a disruptive gang of bullies led by George who would come to the roller skating rink and the miniature golf course at Lake Dunmore, our local hangouts, just to cause trouble.

George wore a cowboy hat, cowboy boots and had a shiny revolver in a holster on his right hip. You could tell he wasn't a normal person. Who walks around in Vermont dressed and acting like Billy The Kid!? As a 10 year old, I had a six shooter cap pistol in a holster, but now I was 17 and, in my mind, very mature and wise—I had graduated to a 22 caliber squirrel rifle and a 20 gauge rabbit shotgun. This guy was clearly off the charts and to be avoided.

One weekend after the camp chores were done a bunch of us brave young men decided, with the help of a beer or two, to go up to the roller skating rink where those Salisbury Bad Assers would be and show them who was boss at Lake Dunmore. We had a leader who was old enough to buy us beer in New York. He was also bigger and stronger than us. So we got him all pumped up with pride as we approached the rink. There was George all decked out in his cowboy apparel. He could tell we meant business as we approached him. He drew his pistol and pointed it at us saying something derogatory about our lineage.

Our leader said, "You think you are pretty tough with that pistol in your hand. Why don't you put it down so we can see how tough you really are." George turned around, handed the pistol to some little guy in back of him, and then came around with his fist and hit our leader so hard the blow knocked him to the ground and broke his jaw. Then George took his pistol in hand, pointed it at our heads and said, "Start running before I shoot you dead!"

My buddies took off like jack rabbits straight into the woods to hide from that Bad Ass George, leaving me alone with that pistol pointed at my forehead. How undignified of my friends to panic and leave me like that! They say in times like this the "fight or flight" response kicks in. Fighting hadn't worked for our leader, and my buddies used up the flight energy, so what was I left with?

To die?

Being too dignified, with a yet undeveloped high IQ, and maybe too proud to show panic in front of the Bad Assers, I slowly turned around and walked away in the direction we had come from, waiting to hear a gunshot as the bullet tore through my body. Going slow kept my heart from beating too fast. If I got shot I would bleed out slower that way.

I don't know what happened to our leader with the broken jaw. Maybe my friends had dragged him into the woods with them. Maybe he got up and somebody took him to the hospital. Maybe George shot him and dumped him in the lake.

Somehow I walked far enough that I began to believe I would survive the terrible experience. Eventually, I made it back to the camp safely, but all my brave friends spent the night lost in the woods, terrified that George was looking for them. When daylight came they were able to find their way back to camp, looking like they had been hit by a Mack truck. Like all young men filled with bravado, we avoided talking about the incident and kept up our appearance of being cool.

I never shared the incident with Agnes. It certainly would have scared the Good Fairy when she realized I wasn't the immaculate boy my mother probably made me out to be. But by the time I walked Agnes back to The Herald we had arranged the prom date. During the few weeks between then and the prom we started seeing each other on the weekends. I remember meeting her mother and father, but that is another tale to tell ...

Prom night came and Agnes was my date. Mom had effectively settled that at the Kong Chow Restaurant in Rutland. For sure Mom had better wisdom when it came to matching me up with girls than I did. Mom judged with wisdom and knowledge while I judged with my eyes.

Even though my mother made me go to Gloria Stanley's Ballroom Dancing classes on Merchants Row, I always tried to avoid dancing. In the late 50s and early 60s ballroom dancing was on the way out and the Jitterbug, Twist, the Watusi and a bunch of new fangled dances were on the way in. Gloria Stanley did not prepare me for "modern" dance, though for some reason she taught us how to play spin the bottle. I did use that once or twice. But the dance lessons must have prepared me for the college prom because during "slow" waltzing songs Agnes danced well by "following," which is like dancing backwards, while I led without stepping on her toes. How do girls do that?

Truthfully, I enjoyed holding her in my arms during the slow dances. There was something about the scent and feel of her breath on my neck that made my nerves tingle. From that night on, anytime I was on the way to her house on Butterfly Avenue in Rutland I would feel the tingling again for the last half mile.

The night before graduation there was a typical college celebration involving a bunch of men gallivanting around town and strutting our stuff—bringing college life to a respectable close and getting ready to launch into the adult world! As often happens on such nights, we had an unexpected incident, an encounter with a young lady who was hitchhiking on the outskirts of town into Randolf. Being fine young gentlemen, we, of course, gave her a ride.

On graduation day the next morning, as I was showing Agnes the boarding house I had lived in, a couple students told me the State Police were looking for me—obviously, as I told Agnes, "To discuss someone else's misbehavior."

When I returned to my room there was a note left on my bed from the young lady our little group had met the night before—my memory of her centers on a mostly toothless smile. She wanted to see me again. I stuffed the note in my pocket before Agnes could see it. I wonder how that note got there? Maybe the State Police delivered it?

According to the story someone told me, at some point during the car ride—and I can neither confirm nor deny the allegation—the young woman claimed one of us honorable young men tossed her purse out the window. Low and behold, according to her there was quite a lot of cash in the purse, and she had reported the entire affair to the State Police. In the end, we got the idea that we should all chip in and reimburse her. We did, it worked, and she was happy. Most importantly, Agnes knew nothing about it and there was peace on the campus *and in my blooming romance.*

So the prom and graduation all happened very nicely. Agnes seemed to really like me and we continued our relationship. It didn't take long to realize she was special, and I wanted our relationship to grow. My goals in life since graduating high school were to get a college degree and a good job, then get married and start a family. I suppose those goals may have been influenced by my mother, alongside TV family shows like Ozzie and Harriet, Father Knows Best, Leave It to Beaver, Brady Bunch, and Andy Griffith.

After graduation I said goodbye to my parents and sisters (and my bedroom) at 105A Grove street in Rutland. I said goodbye to Agnes and headed north to my new life as a "certified" adult. The world and future were mine. Ripe for the picking!!

Several of us college grads were hired by IBM in Essex Junction. We all checked in to the Essex Motel and reported for work the first day. A friend from college and I were told to report to IBM in East Fishkill, NY for training. We had to travel there that day, so we moved out of the Essex Motel and hit the highway. Rooms were reserved for us at the Route 52 Motel in Fishkill.

Moving from Rutland to Essex Junction, only to be told I was now going to work in New York, was a hard change for me. While moving on from college after two years was exciting, and moving from my home and family after 20 years was both exhilarating and heart rending, I felt like a total stranger in this foreign land called New York. I had never traveled outside of Vermont and was so stressed I broke out in hives.

We reported for work the next day and began training—fortunately, two weeks later we were sent back to IBM in Essex Junction, where a few of my friends from college and I rented an apartment on Rte. 15 in Colchester across the road from Fanny Allen Hospital.

Agnes and I continued to see each other on weekends and by July, just a few months later, I had made up my mind that this was the girl I wanted to marry. At a state park in Mendon, we sat on a rock and I told her, "I'm going to ask you to marry me in the near future, so think about it." Was that romantic or what? What was I thinking! Was I giving her a chance to run away so I wouldn't be rejected face-to-face? Or was this my idea of engineering my life and the people in it, now that I had an engineering degree?

At the end of July we were having dinner at the same Chinese Restaurant where we had our first date. I had finally gotten the courage and saved the money to buy a ring. So at dinner I proposed to her, and she accepted. Did I get out of the booth and kneel down as I asked her to marry me? Nope! Never entered my mind. I gave her the engagement ring over a plate of Chicken Chow Mein—and she seemed thrilled. It took years for Agnes to refine me into a proper gentleman.

My birthday was a few days later so I had a very happy birthday that year!

My mother was also very happy to hear we were engaged. She had previously told me the only reason she was alive was to see me graduate from college and marry a good woman. Just three weeks later, on August 19, 1965, Agnes' parents drove her to my apartment to tell me that my mother, Louise Hadley Fiske, had passed away at the Rutland Hospital that morning from a heart attack. She had been admitted a week previous with an angina attack and was being treated with nitroglycerin.

As I heard those words guilt overwhelmed me because I had avoided visiting her in the hospital. I had told my mother that it bothered me to see her there. The guilt turned into anger, and I yelled "I wasn't there" as I put my fist through the wooden door to the apartment bathroom. The next few days were horrible. I returned to my childhood home on Grove Street where my sisters were crying and my father was in such a state of shock he couldn't talk or walk without help. Momma was the love glue that held the family together, and now the family had come undone. As I recall, my sisters were farmed out to relatives and Agnes stood by my side, supportive, as I struggled to "be the man" of the family and care for my father.

Eventually there was a Wake in Middlebury, nearby most of the Fiske family. The funeral was held at the Episcopal Church and the internment at the Weybridge Hill Cemetery. There were three generations of Fiskes in that cemetery. Now there are four.

On January 29, 1966 Agnes and I were married in Rutland at Christ The King Catholic Church on South Main Street, with Monsignor Kennedy presiding. In the following years we had four sons and many adventures…

39 years later, on November 30, 2004 at 12:00 a.m., Rev. Agnes Julia Fiske left this earth to be with her Bridegroom the Lord Jesus Christ.

"And at midnight a cry was heard: 'Behold, the bridegroom is coming; go out to meet him!'"

Matt 25:6

II.

THE CALL TO MINISTRY

Lost & Born Again

"Jesus replied, 'I tell you the truth, unless you are born again, you cannot see the Kingdom of God.'"

John 3:3

At the age of 33 my life was broken and I was lost again. I had a wonderful wife, four precious sons, a new home, a hobby farm, and a great job as a manager at IBM, but I had selfishly wrecked my family. Motivated by an intense desire to be accepted, fit in and belong, my family did not seem to be enough. I wanted more. Extra activities doing civic-minded things helped a little, but frequently kept me away from home. And my wife needed me at home after caring for our children all day. She needed an adult to talk with, a man to support her and help raise a family, but at the time I was unable to do it. Our marriage was quickly veering off the rails, and by July, 1978 it totally crashed and hit bottom.

I was kicked out of our bedroom, told to leave our home the next day and spent the night in the living room unable to sleep. Unable to fix anything and unable to justify myself, it gave me the stark and sobering opportunity to realize I had ruined my marriage. I would be saying goodbye to my sons in the morning as I left my wife after 12 years of marriage, with nowhere to go. A failure cast out into the world to wander alone, afraid and dying inside.

I was lost again!

❖

On Sunday morning at 2:30 a.m., July 2 1978, I wrote a letter to Agnes and God in which I repented for the destruction I had caused. With tears in my eyes, I wrote, "For whatever is left of my life, I want to do it right." I placed the letter on her pillow so she would see it when she awoke.

Expecting to say goodbye to my sons and leave that day, I was supremely surprised that God softened Agnes' heart when she read the letter early in the morning. She said, "Let's wait one more day. Do you still love me?" We made love, and then had coffee on the deck and watched the sunrise bring in the new light.

Our deck was facing south and overlooked a valley and a large beaver pond to the west. It was the longest beaver dam I had ever seen. At the edge of the pond was a beautiful doe and fawn. Throughout my life deer have always been special to see, and the sight of these enchanting creatures added a dimension of charm to the moment.

As I watched the little fawn play at the edge of the water with its mother I had an unforgettable experience—for the first time in my life I heard God speak to me in my mind. He said, "Peter! This is a sign of your new life." I had no doubt that it was God. And I had no doubt that I was being given a new beginning by God and Agnes.

In 1947 an angel from God brought my voice to my mother from the riverbank. In 1978 did that same angel from God whisper in Agnes' ear?

❖

In moving forward with renewed hope for our marriage, Agnes chose to seek counsel from the only clergy we knew in the area, Father Mel Richardson, a priest at Calvary Episcopal Church in Underhill. She called him at 5:30 a.m. and made an appointment for that afternoon. During the meeting Agnes gave her life to Jesus and was born again.

I met with Father Mel the next day. I only remember that he told me to read *1 Corinthians 13*, and no more booze! I went home and found a copy of the *Good News Bible* my sister Becky had left at our house. As I read that chapter God filled me with the love I had lost while living a selfish lifestyle. Love for my wife and children filled and overflowed my heart. Suddenly I was brimming with abundant joy, ascending from the lowest point in my life to a mountain top, touching the heart of God my Father in Heaven. Joy exploded in my heart and radiated into my life in many directions. This intense divine joy lasted for months, and the love has remained permanently.

After meeting with Father Mel Richardson, we began attending Calvary Episcopal Church in Underhill Flats. Calvary was a small mission parish subsidized by the Episcopal Diocese of Vermont. Father Mel was a part-time parish priest and there was no parsonage for him to live in, so he rented an apartment to live in with his family.

Soon thereafter, I was placed in leadership positions at the church. I became a licensed lay minister helping to administer communion and occasionally preached. I was elected to the Vestry, the governing board of church leaders. Eventually, I taught Bible studies and headed up the Evangelism Committee. Agnes was also placed in leadership positions and soon became Senior Warden, the head of the Vestry and confidant for the parish priest.

Studying the Bible and Articles of Religion in the Anglican Book of Common Prayer, I learned the American Episcopal Church had a good Biblical Foundation. But being involved in leadership and observing modern practices and policies of the Episcopal Church in America, I realized the church had drifted away from the Bible and become very liberal. However, God had several families of born-again spirit-filled Christians at Calvary, and as a group we tithed and provided enough funding for the priest to become full-time, and then we purchased a home next door to Calvary as a parsonage for Father Mel and his family.

❖

As I read the Bible and grew in the Lord, I often became so excited I couldn't sleep at night. At such times I would retrieve an artist's paint brush and a small can of paint and paint scriptures, happy faces, Biblical quotes and Peanuts figures on the walls of the bedrooms, bathrooms and hallways. When Agnes woke up in the morning she refused to look at the walls until she had her first cup of coffee. After a while she demarcated a point in the house beyond which I was not allowed to conduct my God-inspired artwork.

As the weeks and months passed, my love for God became intense and passionate as did my love for Agnes and my sons. I was quiet about this experience at IBM because I felt it wise to keep my religious conversion under the radar. I had a humorous thought that someone would discover I was a born again Christian and send me to Africa to evangelize tribes of naked savages running through the jungles with spears. My knowledge of Africa came from movies I had seen as a kid: *Tarzan, Jungle Jim*, and *Bomba The Jungle Boy*.

Rather than sending me to foreign lands, God sent foreigners to minister to me. Jeremiah Karanja came from Kenya dressed in a suit to stoke the fires of evangelism in my heart. Bishop William Johnson came from Pakistan and increased my passion for evangelism. Kevin Graves came from China where he led a large ministry in the underground Christian Church. God also put "senior" Christians in my life who had many years of experience in following the Lord during the Charismatic Renewal time: Jim Hughes, Joe and Maxine Anderson, Pastor Vince Circello, Pastor Pony Pornelus, Pastor Duane Hodgeman, Jody Van Horn, Pastor Ed Hoyt, and many more.

All of these individuals that God sent into my life were for a season and not to be permanent. They came for a time of intense mentoring and influence, then left. One evening I took a walk on Poker Hill Road, a dirt road we lived on, and complained to the Lord about feeling abandoned by these people He put in my life. God spoke to me, saying, "Peter I have sent these people only for a time so that you would learn from them, but not build your life and ministry around them. But I have placed someone in your life who will never abandon or leave you. That is My Holy Spirit."

Then I understood and felt satisfied. I remembered "For I am God, and there is no other; I am God, and there is none like Me, Declaring the end from the beginning, And from ancient times things that are not yet done, Saying, 'My counsel shall stand, And I will do all My pleasure,' Calling a bird of prey from the east, The man who executes My counsel, from a far country. Indeed I have spoken it; I will also bring it to pass, I have purposed it; I will also do it" (*Isaiah 45:5-11*).

This passage heralded my introduction to Bishop William Johnson, a native of Pakistan. A bird of prey who soars over the land looking for resources of food, William came from the East to the US in search of funding resources for his ministry in Pakistan. While in Vermont he stayed in a spare bedroom in our home. Eventually, I became more involved and handled his US donations and bank account.

Ever since this time, my prayer has been: "Lord I give you permission to use my life to serve your purpose on this earth. But use me through my obedience to you and not disobedience." I had read about how God destroyed Pharaoh in Egypt and said to him, "But indeed for this very purpose I have raised you up, that I may show My power in you, and that My name may be declared in all the earth" (*Exodus 9:16).*

"Lord, I give you my life. If it serves your purpose end it, leave it as is or extend it, all for the building up of your Kingdom."

The Shooting Star

As a new Christian I would go out on our deck at night, lay on the bench and look up into the sky and see all the beautiful stars that God had made. If I stayed there long enough I would see shooting stars flash across the sky. One night instead of laying on the deck I went down on the ground where it was sloped, and as I lay there in the grass looking up into the sky my heart was filled with love for my family, for people and especially for God. I told God "I love you," and as I finished that statement a large shooting star with a big tail went zooming across the sky in a big blaze. I knew that God had just answered me and said, "I love you too Peter."

Years later I look back and I understand that God knew that I was going to be there at that moment. God knew that he was going to respond to what I said in the way that he did.

How long ago did God create that meteorite and put it in motion knowing that it was going to connect with me that night? Did God create the meteorite just to answer me that night? Or did God create me and plan my life to be there "for such a time as this"?

How long ago did God know that I was going to exist. How long ago did God plan for me to exist? When did my life begin? At the moment of conception? At physical birth? No, my life began when God decided that I would exist and planned my life.

"For we are God's masterpiece. He has created us anew in Christ Jesus, so we can do the good things he planned for us long ago."

Ephesians 2:10

"God the Father knew you and chose you long ago."

1 Peter 1:2a

"I knew you before I formed you in your mother's womb."

Jeremiah 1:5a

"You saw me before I was born. Every day of my life was recorded in your book. Every moment was laid out before a single day had passed."

Psalm 139:16

A Vision for Evangelism

After praying for God to give me the heart of an evangelist, He began to move in me. In October 1986 one afternoon at IBM I was inspired with a message that I typed onto my computer. From that time on it has been the desire of my heart to accomplish.

The message was:

"Hurting people need God!"

Out of this vision came an outreach letter:

Dear Brothers and Sisters,

Jesus said, "Come unto me all who are heavy burdened and I will give you rest, for my burden is light and my yoke is easy."

Where does a person with a burden go to find Jesus? Jesus is found within His Body (the Church, a community of believers). Within the Church, of which Jesus Christ is the head, He lives and works His purpose, which is to reconcile you and me to God our Father.

If this is true, then we as the Body should throw our nets out into the world and reap the harvest of souls that await us. In so doing our nets will pull in a variety of people. Jesus was found ministering in the streets to all sorts of people. So must we also bring these same people to Jesus.

For each of us there may be people who will be brought to Christ only through us: "Go then, to all peoples everywhere and make them My disciples; baptize them in the name of the Father, Son, and Holy Spirit, and teach them to obey everything that I have commanded you" (Matt 28:19-20a).

"I am the real vine, and my father is the gardener. He breaks off every branch in Me that does not bear fruit, and He prunes every branch that does bear fruit, so that it will be clean and bear more fruit"

(John 15:1-2).

Dare we not obey? Shall we be broken off or shall we be pruned?

What if we could say to people in our communities:
Are you feeling empty inside? Is there something missing in your life, but you don't know what it is?

Have you been unable to find the "happy life" displayed on TV and in movies and magazines? Has the world lied to you, used you, and then forgotten you?

Are you lonely even in a crowd? Are you searching for someone to understand you at the most intimate level?

Have you lost your love of life? Are you filling a hole in your heart with alcohol, sex, drugs, career, materialism, superficial relationships, the latest psycho-fad?

Are you terminally ill and afraid or curious of what is to come?

Are you in trouble? Are you alienated from loved ones or society? Is your past too much too bear?

Would you rather not be alive? Are you filled with hate?

Has poverty or failure destroyed your self-esteem?

Has God been watching over your life, but you don't know Him?

Do you feel a need to understand God's purpose for your life, but you aren't ready to walk into a church?

Without God it is not possible to overcome sin and find inner peace in this life. Without God there is only the grave and eternal destruction ahead of you.

Jesus Christ has made it possible to be reunited with God. He is available to you right now. All you have to do is turn to Him and accept His free gift of salvation.

Would you like to meet someone who has had the same feelings and problems as you, resolved them, and found peace for their life? We will meet with you at your convenience, privately, and in confidence at no cost to you.

We are a Ministry that is offering to help you change the life you have been living. We will not pressure you. You can stop at any time. Our job is only to present you with God's truths and allow you to decide for yourself whether to accept or reject them. There is no harm in trying, but if life continues for you without changing direction, where will it lead you?

Call 899-3403. Ask for a "servant."

"But His word was in my heart like a burning fire Shut up in my bones; I was weary of holding it back, And I could not."

Jeremiah 20:9

With this message burning within me I wanted to initiate a ministry within Calvary Episcopal Church where I was a lay leader. I had been licensed as a Lay Minister, led bible studies, and gave testimonies at times. So I organized an evangelism committee and began preparing other members to evangelize their communities. As such, I wrote up an outline to guide us in our efforts:

The Plan for Bringing Our Community to Christ

On the basis that Jesus is our guide and the head of our Church we can begin this venture in faith.

Our ministry should have the following priorities:

1. Preserve the safety and health of the individual.

2. Begin with reconciliation to God through acceptance of Jesus Christ as Savior and Lord.

3. Present a simple Gospel message based on forgiveness of sins, acceptance of God's work on the cross and Lordship of Jesus Christ.

4. Growth begins with learning Biblical concepts of Christian living.

5. Everything learned must be reinforced through Christian fellowship.

6. Understanding and wisdom are the result of prayer, Biblical study and application.

If you feel that you are entering into a risky situation, ask for help and remember: "Worst case is you might die in service to the Lord. That would make you a martyr and gain you rewards in Heaven."

We begin by giving our message to as many individuals as possible. Remember that giving one message to a person does not get the message to everyone in that household.

During the first contact, after the safety of the individual is ensured, provide a copy of the Bible and some recommended scriptures to read.

Ensure the individual that you are praying for him or her and that many other Christians are praying for him or her while maintaining anonymity. Be prepared to lay hands on him or her in prayer, and, if possible, ask the individual to say the "Sinners Prayer."

At all times encourage and motivate towards prayer, Bible reading, and faith in the promises of God.

The thief on the cross beside Jesus proved that it is never to late for salvation. The conversion of Paul, the woman caught in adultery, and the woman at the well prove that no sin is to great for God to forgive.

The story of Job shows us that for those who have faith in God, although we may lose everything, He can give us a new life better than the first.

Joseph of Arimathea, Lazarus, and Nicodemus show us that fame, position and wealth do not have to keep you from Jesus. God can use these as attributes in His work on earth.

Lazarus shows us that no situation is to hard for God to deal with.

Do not worry about "what if" situations that may arise. Jesus goes with you and is leading you. Prepare yourself with much prayer. Ask God to show you those areas in your life that are blocking your relationship with Him. As they are revealed to you, repent and ask His forgiveness. Allow Him to direct you and be obedient to His commands. If this means repairing broken relationships or righting a wrong, then obey Him and do what you can. This process will give Him a clean vessel to work His purpose.

Most of all do not think that you are not good enough or worthy enough to represent Jesus.

"My Grace is sufficient for you, for My power is perfected in weakness."

2 Corinthians 12:9

Leaving the Episcopal Church

We led Calvary Church using Biblical principles, but eventually our leadership clashed with the Episcopal policies and practices. The end came when the evangelism team I trained was ready to start evangelizing the surrounding towns, but none of us wanted to invite new people to Calvary or any Episcopal Church. Very quickly after that most of the born-again Christians left Calvary and went in different directions. My direction led us into 18 months of intense leadership training that God had in store for us in Morrisville with the Community Gospel Church.

Leaving the Episcopal Diocese of Vermont was a hard decision because from my early teen years the Trinity Episcopal Church in Rutland was a very important part of my life. As an infant I had been baptized by Father Harvey Butterfield who eventually became the 6th Bishop of the Episcopal Diocese of Vermont, from 1961 to 1974. I was Confirmed by Bishop Vedder Van Dyk and spent my summers at Rockpoint Episcopal Conference Center in Burlington. I would be a camper for one week, then the dishwasher for the rest of the summer.

On the other hand my passion for the Word of God and my love for Jesus Christ was all consuming. There was no question for me. The hurtful part was leaving the people I had grown to love.

Morrisville

After leaving Calvary Episcopal Church I was asked by a Vestry member why I left. He wanted a formal explanation, so I wrote one with 13 points of contention.

Leaving was hard, like a divorce, because I had spent 11 years growing in the Lord there and I loved the people. However, God led me to the Community Gospel Church in Morrisville where a friend named DL from IBM was attending and told me about their mission trips to South America. Little did I know that God had prepared a special "Boot Camp" for my development as a Christian Leader. My learning ability has never been from books or teachers. I learn best through trial and error.

The Church had a great worship ministry with modern Christian songs, not from a hymnal with music dating back 200 years. There were prophetic messages during worship, people praying in tongues with interpretation. The preaching was not being read from a script, and the prayers were not being read from The Book of Common Prayer. This was a new experience for my wife Agnes and I, and it seemed to be people in genuine worship of the Lord.

We heard the term shepherding used to explain the leadership structure in the church. The shepherds were on the high mountains watching for danger as the sheep lived down below on the sides of hills grazing. The sheep followed the shepherds from pasture to pasture in the safety of their care.

I asked one of the elders if I could discuss shepherding with him. I knew he was experienced as a leader and I loved listening to him share his experiences. But he looked startled when I mentioned shepherding and said I would have to meet with the pastor to discuss it.

After this God opened our eyes to red flags of warning.

We were basically told, "If you don't submit to the pastor, you won't be able to submit to God. You will be referred to as unrighteous and shunned."

This message clearly went against the grain of Scripture:

> "Then Jesus shouted out again, and he released his spirit. At that moment the curtain in the sanctuary of the Temple was torn in two, from top to bottom." (*Matt 27:50-52*)

God makes unequivocally clear that the path to Him is not through the pastor, but through Jesus:

> "For there is one God and one Mediator between God and men, the Man Christ Jesus" (*1 Timothy 2:5*).

The curtain was opened for us to come directly to God through Jesus. Jesus is our mediator. We don't need to come to a priest or pastor as a way to God. Jesus is the Way!

Another alarming trend was that the pastor was good at bringing women into submission to him. He would turn wives against their husbands to get the husbands to submit to him. This happened to DL at a time when the church was meeting in the second story of DL's garage.

Once again, according to the Bible, this method is deceitful, underhanded and the opposite of what Jesus taught:

> Jesus replied. "But from the beginning of the creation, God 'made them male and female. For this reason a man shall leave his father and mother and be joined to his wife, and the two shall become one flesh'; so then they are no longer two, but one flesh. Therefore what God has joined together, let not man separate" (*Mark 10: 6-9*).

To implement Jesus' instruction, during marriage ceremonies I state: "For as much as this couple has pledged their love and sealed their vows before God and this assembly, I charge that under God no one should seek to weaken or harm this union; may God be an enemy to its enemies, and a friend to its friends. Therefore, what God has joined together, let not man separate."

The pastor put forward misleading teachings on tithing. He claimed, "The Bible teaches triple tithe." However, nowhere does the Bible put a percentage on the amount on gifts and offerings. We are encouraged to be cheerful givers. A tithe of the first fruits of our labor is understood to be 10% of the gross.

According to the pastor, only he or elders were qualified to give advice and counsel. What we said to people in the church was repeated to the pastor and he would criticize us for what we said and tell us we were not to advise or counsel people.

The Word of God tells us that such a narrow-minded view of who can give advice is untrue:

"And He Himself gave some to be apostles, some prophets, some evangelists, and some pastors and teachers, for the equipping of the saints for the work of ministry, for the edifying of the body of Christ" (*Ephesians 4:11-12*)

My friend DL left the church, and after a year his wife left also. Their two daughters stayed and were not allowed to have contact with their "unrighteous" parents. Their older daughter was cohabitating with the pastor because he prophesied that she was going to be his new wife. This happened after he had prophesied that his first wife was terminally ill. She submitted to him, went to bed and waited to die. After a long period of time she realized she was not dying and eventually escaped from the church and her husband. She went into hiding with a new name and cut all ties with the church to maintain her safety. Today she is living with one of her daughters and attending a Bible-believing, Spirit-filled church where her daughter is part of the worship team.

One man in the church, who was very damaged from childhood, received an inheritance of $60,000 when his father died. The pastor and elders "borrowed" all of it from the man and never paid it back. Years later he contacted me after deciding to leave the church. I was able to refer him to a Christian counselor in his town.

Morrisville Struggles – The End

Thus says the Lord God to the shepherds:

> Woe to the shepherds of Israel who feed themselves! Should not the shepherds feed the flocks? You eat the fat and clothe yourselves with the wool; you slaughter the fatlings, *but* you do not feed the flock. The weak you have not strengthened, nor have you healed those who were

sick, nor bound up the broken, nor brought back what was driven away, nor sought what was lost; but with force and cruelty you have ruled them.

Behold, I *am* against the shepherds, and I will require My flock at their hand; I will cause them to cease feeding the sheep, and the shepherds shall feed themselves no more; for I will deliver My flock from their mouths, that they may no longer be food for them. *Ezekiel 34:2b-4,10.*

Messages from the LORD in response to prayer:

8-3-90

PW presented the church with an offer to buy the Station House Restaurant in Morrisville. The elders were looking for direction from all of us on the project. The restaurant would be a place where our people could work and be a public witness. I was opposed to the sale of alcoholic beverages. I also felt that Pastor John presented it as a surprise to himself, but during Phil's talk it appeared that it was planned months in advance.

At the evening service God spoke to Agnes and told her that she had pulled away from her brothers and sisters there in the last few weeks and that she was sinning. Agnes was led to address the fellowship and repent and ask forgiveness. She received many hugs that night. This preceded the Lord's Supper. Very appropriate timing from God.

"Create in me a clean heart, oh God" (*Psalm 51:10*).

8-6-90

I felt that God was telling me not to participate in PW's plan for a restaurant: "Also you shall not go into the house of feasting to sit with them, to eat and drink" (*Jeremiah 16:8*).

8-7-90

Agnes and I met with Pastor John and discussed tithing vs New Testament giving and also submission to civil authority. I also shared with Pastor John that I felt that God was telling me not to participate in the restaurant (*Jer 16:8*).

Jim Hughes ministered to me during supper at The Peking Duck restaurant in Winooski. A scripture kept coming to him, the story from *Ezekiel 8* where God shows Ezekiel a hole in the wall of the temple and tells him to go through. Ezekiel goes through and finds a door. He opens the door and sees all the hidden abominations inside. God does not require Ezekiel to do anything other than to see. Jim urged that if and when I leave Community Gospel Church it must be in peace. I must be obedient to Scripture and respect the authority of the elders.

I believe God was telling me I was in Morrisville only to observe and for Him to put things into my heart for His use. He is in charge of His people and is their shepherd. He will change what needs changing and correct what needs correcting.

8-30-90

Over the radio Agnes received *Ezekiel 8* as an example of how we are to leave the correction of leaders up to the Lord, rather than to try to do it ourselves.

In early September while mowing the lawn I was distressed to the point of tears about our situation with Community Gospel Church. I needed God's help but I didn't even know what to pray. I did not know what to pray for except for God's will to prevail in my life. I did not know if I was to stay or leave the church in Morrisville. I felt helpless and hopeless. Suddenly I began to pray in tongues, in a language I had never used before.

9-4-90

Jim Hughes had given me a copy of *A Tale of Three Kings* that prepared me for a meeting with Pastor John that night. I knew that God did not want me to oppose Pastor John. Do not raise a hand against God's anointed. The meeting was extremely peaceful, and at a point where Agnes thought we might start talking about leaving, God audibly spoke to her, "It is not time."

9-18-90

I met with Pastor John alone and tried to tell him that I could not submit to the system and that God was going to move us out of Morrisville.

In response he communicated the following points of contention:

1) The only way I could leave in a Biblically correct manner was to be sent out.

2) The only way anyone in the Bible went anywhere was to be sent out, and then return to the Church.

3) I needed to consult the elders on decisions like accepting the Walk to Emmaus assignment and going fishing on the weekend. Trying to make me feel guilty, Pastor John said he could not give his message that Sunday because the whole body was not there—as Duey and I were absent.

4) If I had consulted the elders in both cases and gotten their counsel and then determined that God wanted me to go, the church could have been praying for me.

5) He claimed my theology was wrong, but he wouldn't discuss it with me because I had a weakness towards intellectualism that cut me off from Biblical principles!

6) He emphasized his credentials as a mature Christian to legitimize his God given authority over me.

7) He told me it was not right to have a relationship with God that did not include the counsel of others—otherwise I could fall into error.

As I was leaving that night he told me that I scared him. He had seen too many people think that they knew God and didn't need anyone else. They went off and were lost.

Sept 28

Agnes and I met with the elders, and they repeated a lot of the same things for Agnes' sake. They seemed to be more in tune with Pastor John. They insisted that we needed to stay and work out our salvation there.

Afterward we knew that we could not stay and submit to that system.

Since Pastor John had said that he would no longer meet with me and I needed to meet with the elders, I made an appointment with the elders to inform them that we would not return to Community Gospel Church. I arrived in town early with 20 minutes to spare before the meeting. I parked nearby and grabbed my Bible. God told me to read *John 16:1-6*

> These things I have spoken to you, that you should not be made to stumble. They will put you out of the synagogues; yes, the time is coming that whoever kills you will think that he offers God service. And these things they will do to you because they have not known the Father nor Me. But these things I have told you, that when the time comes, you may remember that I told you of them.

This scared me because I knew the pastor and elders carried handguns for protection. There had been threats on the life of the pastor from relatives of members who were not allowed to have contact with "unrighteous people."

Were they going to shoot me? Why did God have me read that? He knew it would scare me. I went to the meeting believing I might be killed because it was important that I was obedient to God rather than let fear control me.

The elders didn't shoot me and I left in peace, but they were leaving the door open for me to return so that I could work out my salvation at Community Gospel Church. In their view, I was walking away and losing my salvation.

In leaving, my time of God-ordained training in this church came to an end, and God gave me this verse from *Exodus 3:20* "When you leave you will not go empty handed." I left with knowledge, experience and wisdom in being a better shepherd for God.

The Trip

In December 1989, while driving home from Rutland, Agnes had a small accident. A car backed out of a parking place and into the side of our truck while she was stopped in traffic. The truck was dented, but not seriously damaged.

At the end of January our daughter in law, who lived in Hawaii with our son Chris, went into early labor. She was only six and a half months pregnant. The doctors were able to stop the labor with medication and she stabilized well enough to go home, but would not be able to exert herself at all. Before she went home we recognized that she and Chris would need help. Chris could get two weeks leave, but would need help to take care of their son Christopher and keep up the house.

At this time the insurance settlement came and provided enough pay for Agnes to go to Hawaii where she would help Chris and his family for a month. Agnes told her mother about the upcoming trip, and she told Agnes to come to Rutland so she could give her $110 to spend for the trip. Agnes used some of the money to buy some clothes she would need in Hawaii, but saved the remainder.

After buying the plane ticket there was enough left over from the insurance settlement for Agnes and me to spend two nights in St Jean Quebec for our anniversary, during which we had a wonderful time. However, during this time, the prospect of leaving me for a month hit Agnes and she became distraught, shedding many tears. Agnes spoke at length to God, imploring Him to "fix things" so that she wouldn't have to be separated from me for a month. By Saturday, Agnes was ready to explode with emotion. Sunday morning in the shower she sought the Lord for direction, and He clearly told her to "Go and do!" She took this as a command and accepted in obedience, but continued to grieve.

At church that day she gave a testimony about what was going on in her life and how she was going into a house where she would have to be in the role of a submissive servant to her son and his wife. She related how God had been working and developing a gentle and peaceful spirit in her for a few months—and that this would help her carry out the assignment. She also said that she believed God was sending her to light a spiritual fire within Chris and Alena. After the service everyone in the church gathered round and laid hands on her in prayer, during which it was prophesied that God would be with Agnes when she set foot on the soil of Hawaii.

This reminded me of a prophecy Agnes had given during worship in October: "If we share the gospel with others with all our heart, the roots of the trees will tremble where we walk."

This strengthened her greatly, but the tears kept coming.

On Monday a Christian friend from our Bible study told me that he and his wife had prayed and decided they would pay our phone bill while Agnes was in Hawaii so we could talk every day. They thought it was important that we do that. I met Agnes at the grocery store after work and told her. She started crying in front of the frozen veggies.

I should have waited.

Wednesday at midnight Lee knocked on our bedroom door and asked me to come out to the living room so he could talk to me. He said he had been praying and decided Mom should not go because he could see the pain she was going through. After seeing our marriage flourish since we left the Episcopal church, he thought we should not be apart for so long. Therefore, he decided that he should be the one to go—even though this would cost him his job.

God gave me wisdom, and I told Lee that it was a fine thing for him to be at a point in his faith where he was willing to sacrifice himself like that, but God had told Mom to "Go and do!" and we understood this to be His will and command. Therefore, Mom had to go. Only God could change that now. I also told him there was a possibility that they would still need help after Mom left and that at that time God might want Lee to go. So we agreed to pray and seek God's will for the situation.

On Thursday a Christian friend stopped by to visit Agnes. She told Agnes that she had been praying for her and believed God had revealed to her that I would be going to Hawaii also. But, of course, there was no way I

The Call to Ministry   67

could afford that without going into considerable debt.

Within minutes the phone rang and it was Agnes' mother saying that on Saturday she was bringing up $300 for Agnes to take with her for spending. Agnes' friend cautioned her that maybe Satan was setting her up for disappointment. Now Agnes was on an emotional roller coaster, not knowing how to properly handle her thoughts and what to hope for—even with the extra money it would cost more than $300 for me to go.

When I got home Agnes told me what happened and the turmoil she was going through. God gave me wisdom and I shared with her that I thought the only acceptable attitude was to accept the trip and the possibility of a month's separation. God wanted her to be obedient and to accept the hardship and suffering that went along with it. If He wanted to intercede, He would do it on His own initiative, not by ours.

We went to the Labrie's for supper that night and, on the way, I delivered Lee's car to Kathy Aires. She bought it for $800. The next morning Lee told us that we could use $450 of his money to send me or whoever God decided to Hawaii. I told him that we could only accept money that was obviously from God. Lee was acting out of his compassion and not as a prompting from God.

While we were at the Labrie's, Agnes shared about her friend and the $300. Duey asked if the only thing holding me from going was the "lack of resources." I knew that out of brotherly compassion he would offer to help with some money. So I said that it would be easy for me to get the money on my own power, but that it had to be obviously from God. Otherwise, I couldn't accept it. That was the only way I would know for sure that God wanted me to go.

At the house meeting later that night Agnes shared her struggle with Brian and Matt and asked them to pray and ask God to intercede and send me to Hawaii also.

Friday morning Agnes' mother called and said that she was bringing up $400 instead of $300. Agnes told me this over the phone and I started to get excited that God was going to finish it and provide all the money. Agnes was really in turmoil again because she believed I might be looking at this wrongly and not recognize a gift from God and reject it as coming from human compassion instead of from God. I told her I had faith that God would be able to handle me and not allow that to happen. I also told her that, on faith, I was going to inform my manager that I might need vacation time for a trip to Hawaii.

I had lunch with another Christian friend who told me that he and his wife had prayed and felt God wanted them to donate towards our trip so they could share in our ministry to our family. On this basis I accepted $100. Now I really got excited and, on faith, reserved seats on a flight for March 1. There was only one seat left on the plane from Chicago to Hawaii.

Another sign from God.

With $500 committed towards the trip I called Agnes and told her I was convinced that it was a go and that I had reservations on March 1, returning with her on March 13. She told me we had received an insurance check for $7.83 in the mail. No idea why. Another sign from God. Then she remembered that she had money left over from the first gift from her mother which, instead of $110, turned out to be $200.

Agnes said she had about $130 left. WOW. The tickets for my reservation were $638 and we had $637.83 in unsolicited gifts. I said that we had enough empty soda bottles in the cellar to make up the 17 cents. But when I got home Agnes took the money out of her pocketbook and counted out $131. We now had $638.83.

I guess the 83 cents is spending money or what you call an abundance of God's blessing. It covered a cup of coffee at O'Hare Airport in Chicago.

Agnes also informed me that Alena had told her that by the first week in March she should be well enough to return to normal. She would not need help beyond the time that Agnes would be there. So, God had resolved everything. We were anxious to see what purpose He had beyond the obvious physical help that Chris and Alena needed.

The LORD our GOD is AWESOME!

Later Friday night Nathan offered to help out with spending money.

Out of all this we are discovering how much more awesome God is than we ever knew and that He is definitely Lord of our lives and has purpose for us that will not fail. We are also learning that people we have ministered to in the past are being used by God to minister to us now. And that people we have been praying for are within the power of God to do with as He pleases—such as Agnes' mother, who on Friday explained to Agnes that she believed in God but had a lot of bitterness towards Him because "bad things happen to people and the wicked seem to prosper."

Obviously, God is working on her!

Ho! He is so awesome! He loves and cares for us!

I feel compelled to record all these happenings because I don't think God wants them lost from memory.

Update 2-24-90

Alena had the baby early and everything was okay! She would be able to return home in 3 days and would be back to normal that week. Therefore, Agnes' physical job seemed to be over. She called and said we should consider her coming home and cancelling my trip and whatever money was left we could give it to Chris and Alena.

We decided to pray about it.

The next morning was Sunday, and I went to Church. The teachings and testimonies shared that day all related to keeping our lives focused on God and not let what is happening in the physical world lead us away from God's purpose for us. That confirmed in me that Agnes' physical job was done in Hawaii, but her real reason for going which was God's plan was not completed yet.

We should continue as planned.

That same morning on the way to the hospital to visit Alena and the baby, Chris turned on the radio to a Christian radio station. The preacher was preaching how we should not let what is going on physically change God's plan.

Later we talked on the phone and since we both had prayed and then heard the same message, we felt it was God telling us to continue with the plan He had for us.

❖

I arrived in Hawaii on Thursday, March 1. That Saturday Agnes and I travelled to the north shore of the island and parked near a beach where the surfers go for the big surf. We walked around for ten minutes, and when we returned the car had been broken into and Agnes' purse and all the gifts we bought that day had been stolen. Our return flight airlines tickets and a pair of eyeglasses had been in the purse and were also now gone.

We reported the crime to the police and the airline. The next day we all went back to search for the purse, thinking the thieves would have taken the cash and other valuables, then trashed the rest. We combed the roadsides and other parking areas and found nine other purses and bags that had been stolen and discarded in the grass and bushes—but not a sign of Agnes' purse!

As we looked for her purse I had a prompting from the Lord to stop and talk with the two cops who were going through the ones we had found. I witnessed to my faith and one of them said that another cop who was a Christian had been working on him for a year. He suggested that maybe God had sent me to find these purses for other people and also to talk to him. Soon the Christian cop came along, and we met and talked. He said to the first cop, "See! All Christians don't have brown skin." He was of Asian descent.

Later that day on the radio and again that evening at church Agnes and I heard the message that we should not be "results-oriented." We should be "obedience-oriented" and satisfied to carry out God's command without expecting specific outcomes.

On Sunday Chris recommended that we go to a nearby church in Pearl City. As we entered the church we notice we were the only white people there. We were greeted warmly and given white sea shell necklaces to wear. Obviously the necklaces identified us as first time visitors.

The pastor introduced himself to us and we explained that we were from Vermont visiting our son and his family because his wife was hospitalized and in danger if losing her life and baby.

During the service the pastor interrupted his sermon and prophesied to me saying, "The brother from Vermont! God is doing great things in your life and new things are coming! You need to be ready."

We thought we had come to instigate a spiritual fire in Chris and Alena, but it wasn't happening. On Friday night I couldn't sleep and felt that God wanted me to spend time with Him so I got out of bed and read the Bible and prayed. I was also prompted to rebuke Satan from interfering with our purpose. I got up and in Jesus' name rebuked Satan and his spirits out of every room in the apartment and also laid hands on my grandson, Christopher, who was sleeping. Then I went back to the Bible and immediately came to *Zacharia 1:8* which God had given me in November, as a result of praying for Him to reveal His plan to me for my life. I then remembered God had continued that message in a dream and a revelation on January 10.

As I read *Zacharia 1:1-3*, I felt God wanted me to deliver this scripture to Corporal Greg Nails. In August of 1989, Chris talked to Greg, a backslidden

Christian, and told him the spiritual history of our family. It prompted the young man to recommit his life to the Lord and write me a letter encouraging me in changing churches. At that time we were involved with Community Gospel Church in Morrisville, which was very cultish, and I was preparing to leave.

Chris told me that he thought Greg had backslidden again. I called him the next day and made an appointment to meet with him on Sunday. When we met he mentioned that two weeks prior he had come across a letter I had written him and, somehow, knew I was coming to Hawaii. After sharing with him how I came to be in Hawaii and that speaking to him seemed to be the top priority for God, he acknowledged that God was truly calling him to repent. As tears swelled in his eyes he excused himself and went to the bathroom. Upon returning he told me he had been close to getting involved in something very bad, but now he was repenting from that.

As we parted that day Greg was determined to answer God's call. He also felt prompted to bless me and gave me $80. Believing God was prompting him, I accepted it. That was my first pay for ministry!

The last night we were in Hawaii, God revealed to me that, just as we had searched for our lost purse and found others, we had also searched for the souls of our children and found another's. God was in control all the way, and He wanted me to know that all I needed to do was to be obedient to Him. I need not struggle for the results that I expect, just be obedient and accept His results and His blessings.

I know that God will deal with all our children and that it will be His plan and not ours.

An interesting additional blessing is that the church Chris led us to in Hawaii was the one in which Greg Nails had been saved in 1987.

How awesome God is!

In His Name.

Marriage Encounter & Cursillo

Since we had come to Mel Richardson and Calvary Episcopal Church in a marital crisis, Mel signed us up for a Marriage Encounter weekend in New Hampshire. It was a great weekend led by Brother Bob White at a Monastery in Enfield.

At the weekend we learned and practiced the basics of good marital communication. We also had opportunities to share our story with the group and, in more detail, with the leaders, Linda and George Quinn. Because we were willing to tell our story we were invited back to more weekends as a team couple. Since they thought we were good speakers, we were recruited for more leadership activities with Marriage Encounter.

After Marriage Encounter we were signed up for the men's and women's Cursillo Weekends, a crash course in Christianity that promised "an encounter with oneself, Christ, and others." We both accepted the invitation to go deeper with God. I attended the men's weekend, and two weeks later Agnes went to the women's weekend.

Over the weekend I learned much about Christianity and listened to many speakers share their personal testimonies and experiences. I became so inspired and filled with God's Holy Spirit that when I returned home Agnes couldn't stand listening to me and began to doubt if she should go to her weekend.

For most of my life I had been antisocial and disliked most people. But at this weekend I was overwhelmed with an experience of shared love with others, and realized that for the first time in my life there was a place I belonged with people who loved me. What's more, they had to love me "Because the Bible said so!"

Agnes came back from her weekend as filled with the Spirit and love for others as I'd been, and soon we became team speakers on Cursillo weekends. My involvement with Cursillo led to an invitation to help staff the first men's Kairos weekend, which is Cursillo redesigned for incarcerated people.

I had turned down opportunities to be involved in prison ministry a few times—because it wasn't what I wanted to do *and even the thought of it was scary*. I had visited an employee a few times when he was incarcerated, and that was not enjoyable at all. But, as is usually the case, God was silently guiding me in an unexpected direction. I agreed to be on the Kairos team because I had vowed that I would go anywhere at anytime to talk about God and share my personal testimony of how I became a Christian.

Kairos is the Greek word for God's time, as distinct from Chronos, which is man's chronological clock time—that can be measured in seconds, minutes, hours, years. Kairos is also used to depict God's timing, the *right* moment, the opportune moment. The perfect time chosen by God and not scheduled or measured by man.

Little did I know, God would use Kairos to change my life so completely.

Chronos Vs. Kairos

The best living example of the difference between Kairos and Chronos for me occurred in 1966 when Agnes' doctor said, "You are pregnant and the baby will be due in mid-January."

We were living in an apartment in Burlington on Convent Square. I was in the National Guard, waiting to go to bootcamp and then AIT training as a Medic. Our guard unit commander agreed to wait until after the baby was born in mid-January before sending me to boot-camp for basic training. So I told our landlord the baby would be born mid-January and we would move out then. The plan was for Agnes to go live in Rutland with her parents on Butterfly Avenue while I was away for 6 months of military training.

As mid-January approached on the "Chronos" calendar we realized that the baby was going to be late! Stupid doctor made a huge mistake!!!

I told the landlord we couldn't move out because the baby was going to be late. He said, "I already rented your apartment to my sister-in-law and she is moving in on January 17. So, you have to move out!"

So we moved into a motel room at the Champlain Motor Lodge on Route 7 in Shelburne. In recent years that motel has become a homeless shelter funded by the state. We were kind of homeless in 1967.

We celebrated Agnes' 21st birthday in a motel room. I took her out for dinner at a nearby restaurant where we had eaten a year before on our wedding night. Agnes was able to have her first "legal" cocktail, a Manhattan.

On Friday the 13th 1967 we woke up at the motel to the coldest day of the year. Over 30 below zero and my car, a 61 Plymouth Newport, would not start. It took me all day to get it started—just in time for Agnes to proclaim "My water just broke." She went into the bathroom, I went out and started the car. I came back in expecting to rush her to the hospital but she was busy fixing her hair, putting on makeup, and in my mind about to have the baby any moment.

Eventually we got to the hospital and hours later our son Christopher was born. The "gender reveal" was when the nurse put the baby in my arms in the waiting room and said, "It's a boy."

That was a Kairos moment!

The next day I left for basic training at Fort Polk, LA. Chronos time then kicked in for 20 weeks until I returned home.

Dream: January 10, 1990

In the dream I left my house with two friends to go for a walk in the woods. At first, we walked on a road that went through my neighbor's land, then we left the road and walked on the lawn next to his house. There were other people on his lawn who belonged there. We went through one small out-building, perhaps a shed, and into a large multi-storied barn, then up a flight of stairs. There were empty cots throughout the barn where old men had been sleeping.

The first phase of the dream ended, and I found myself once again walking on the neighbor's road. This time I was alone. I saw deer in a field to the right and went into the field to watch them. They ran off a short ways, then stopped to graze near a small cluster of apple trees. In the middle of the field was a large, flat, slanted rock that I was able to lay against while I watched the deer.

Then my neighbor came into the field with a few workers and began to work. I think they were preparing beds. The rock I was laying on turned into a bed. I was laying on it awake and fully clothed, leaning on my elbow. The neighbor turned and noticed me with a start. I asked him if he minded me being there and he said it was OK. Then his 12 year old son came over and asked me questions that tested my knowledge of God.

I knew the correct answers.

The dream ended, and I awoke and got out of bed. After showering and shaving, I reviewed my notes from the previous night's teaching.

Suddenly, God's revelation struck me like a thunderbolt: as He had delivered the Hebrews out of bondage in Egypt, He also delivered me out of bondage to sin when I repented and He heard my cry. As He had led the Hebrews through the Red Sea and out of the old life forever, He also led me away from the old life and through the waters of baptism. As He had led the Hebrews through the desert until the old generation that still had the memory of life in Egypt died, so He also was leading me through sanctification as the old flesh was dying and falling away. As He had pulled His people out of oppression by foreign governments and into His remnant, He also pulled me out of oppression in the Episcopal church and into His remnant.

God's presence was on me and I lay down on my bed, incredulous and weeping because He had shown me that I was part of His complex and awesome plan. Agnes came in and, after I explained what was happening, told me about the revelation she had a few days earlier:

"I realized that you and I were not propagating two different ministries, but that we were one ministry—together. There wasn't any more being on this or that committee and spreading out what God had given us as special gifts. While it seemed like we were going in two different directions, God reminded me that you have always been able to work with people under any circumstance, a wonderful gift that works in harmony with the gifts God has given me in reaching out and ministering to people. What great joy filled me when God revealed to me that he has truly given us a ministry of serving together; a joy beyond words or description."

During that day my son Lee had been fasting and praying that I would get an assignment at IBM. In the afternoon God let Lee know that he didn't need to fast and pray for me any more, as I had received the assignment.

That day I also told God I was trusting Him for an interpretation of the dream. I was certain the dream was from Him because it was still so vivid in my memory. The only other dream I had ever experienced like that was one in which Adam with short hair was standing on a low platform in a large room. He was surrounded by young people like him and recommitting his life to the Lord. The short hair came true. I saw the room and platform at the Grange hall in Morrisville, and Adam interpreted the dream to mean that God was telling me to trust in Him for Adam's salvation because He would accomplish it.

The day after the dream, I received an interpretation of the first part of the dream while we were in our house-meeting singing a song about the return of the Messiah: "The dead in Christ shall rise first" (*1 Thess 4:13-18.*) As I was searching for this scripture, I came across another passage: "Behold I come like a thief! Blessed is he who stays awake and keeps his clothes with him, so that he may not go naked and be shamefully exposed" (*Rev 16:15*).

The empty beds where old men had been sleeping meant that the dead in Christ had risen. In the field, the Lord returned to gather those who were left, and I was there and ready. He gave me permission to be there. I went before the Lord and was accepted as a Christian. God has shown me that this can happen in my lifetime. I believe that He wants me to believe it in preparation for serving Him, now and in the future.

On Wednesday, 1-24-90, Adam indicated that he and Amy may be open to Church and Bible study. Praise God! Another dream coming true as God is helping me work out the interpretation of my latest dream. His way of saying, "Pay attention to my promises."

On February 10, we had a family dinner because Agnes was going to Hawaii the next day. Lee, Nathan and Robbie, Adam and Amy and her baby Joshua were there. Adam informed us that Anne Nichols had visited, and during the visit he had become upset and yelled while trying to change Joshua because no one helped him. After this Anne had told Amy that when Joshua got older Adam would probably beat him. This upset them both so much they decided that Joshua should be brought up in a Christian atmosphere.

They had also been discussing Revelation and the signs of the times, reaching the conclusion that we are now in the end times. As a result of this Adam said they had decided to take us up on our offer to do a Bible study with them. Agnes would stop by once a week during the day and do a homemakers study with Amy, and Amy said that when Agnes returned from Hawaii she wanted to visit our church in Morrisville.

Praise God!

My dream of Adam recommitting his life to the Lord is coming true step by step—and this is happening at a time that I am still dealing with my dream of end times.

At church on February 11, I shared much of this with Martin and he directed me to *Habakkuk 2:2-3*: "Then the LORD replied, 'Write down the revelation and make it plain on tablets so that a herald may run with it. For the revelation awaits an appointed time; it speaks of the end and will not prove false. Though it linger, wait for it; it will certainly come and will not delay.'"

On February 27, Adam recommitted his life to Jesus Christ and also announced his engagement to Amy. Praise God!

While Agnes was in Hawaii and I was still in Vermont, I told her about the scripture that Martin had given me from Habakkuk. She told me that she had received that same scripture from God to give to me, but had forgotten to. She even had it noted and dated in her bible.

Wow!

Peace

"Be anxious for nothing, but in everything by prayer and supplication, with thanksgiving, let your requests be made known to God; and the peace of God, which surpasses all understanding, will guard your hearts and minds through Christ Jesus."

Philippians 4:6-7

Sitting in a recliner in the living room at 3 a.m., I was unable to reconcile the impending marriage of my son Adam to the wrong woman. I knew she was not right for him, and it could only end in disaster. We had tried talking to them, tried to teach them the principles of living a Christian lifestyle. We had invited them into our Bible study and they both committed their lives to the Lord—but, on her part, it was all phony. She was only seeking approval to marry our son. We both saw through her machinations and knew it was wrong.

My mind raced through all the scenarios I could imagine to stop the marriage. I tried praying, but couldn't concentrate enough to do it. I was so upset I couldn't even read the Bible. I was out of control and in need of help. All I could do was sit there with tear-filled eyes feeling helpless, my mind subjected to the cruel visions of a most dreadful marriage that played out over and again in my imagination.

I got up out of my seat and went to the dining room table, then opened the Bible to a random page and began to read out loud. My mind began to settle down and I was able to concentrate on the Biblical verse. It was from one of the gospels:

Then he got into the boat and his disciples followed him. Without warning, a furious storm came up on the lake, so that the waves swept over the boat. But Jesus was sleeping. The disciples went and woke him, saying, "Lord, save us! We're going to drown!" He replied, "You of little faith, why are you so afraid?" (*Matthew 8:23-27*).

It was as if Jesus was there speaking directly to me, saying, "You of little faith, why are you so afraid? Don't you know that I am in control of your son's life? Leave him to Me." His words cut to the core of my heart and restored me with conviction in Him, with faith and trust in His infinite power and benevolence.

I was not in control. God was.

I read on:

Then he got up and rebuked the winds and the waves, and said "Peace be still!" and it was completely calm. The men were amazed and asked, "What kind of man is this? Even the winds and the waves obey him!" (*Matthew*)

In the wake of reading these words I felt a warm blanket of peace come down from above and cover me. I became immediately relaxed and sleepy, then went into the bedroom and turned off all the lights. It was a very dark night and as I slipped under the covers I noticed a faint green-blue glow on my left arm that extended about an inch from my skin. Being technically-minded by default (not always catching the spiritual clues), I thought, *That's interesting. My skin is glowing. I wonder what phenomenon caused that?*

Then I fell fast asleep.

The next day I remembered the glow on my skin and became excited when I remembered what happened just prior to it. I recalled a passage in the Bible wherein Moses glowed after encountering the presence of God on Mount Sinai, and realized the blue-green glow on my arm was the presence of God covering me with peace.

After this revelation I never again became so worried about my son. The situation did not change and he did get married, *and* it did end in disaster. Within three years they were divorced with two children caught in the maelstrom between them. It was a very painful experience for all of us. But deep down I remembered that God was in charge of my son, not me. Showing me this was one of the most loving things God has ever done for me. As time goes on I have been able to retain much of that peace, and I appreciate it more.

Problems still come, but I handle them better now that I realize I'm not God.

God is God!

It All Comes Together, 1991

A couple nights after Bishop William Johnson from Pakistan Gospel Assemblies left I was in my screen tent asking the Lord to show me what He was doing in my life. I felt like my dream the previous year needed to be reinterpreted to give me a better sense of its meaning. I had just read in John Carr's book *Visions* that God would not give a dream or vision unless He wanted it understood, and I believed God was telling me it was time to understand the dream.

Suddenly, I realized that the rock in my dream was just like the one in my back yard, where I sit and sometimes stand to pray at night. The deer in my dream represented the doe and twin fawns that live in the small woods in back of our house. They frequently visit our lawn in the back yard. In the dream they had been grazing beneath apple trees. Taking the hint, last year after the dream I had planted 5 apple trees, then planted six more this year in our back yard.

The landowner and workers coming into the field were God, The Lord of The Harvest, and people like Jeremiah, William and Kevin who had visited my house. As in the dream, I had been given permission to be there with them and join them in the harvest work.

Other things coming to my remembrance were:

1. Agnes' prophecy: "If we share the Gospel with our hearts, even the roots of the trees will tremble wherever we walk."
2. In asking God about the timing to approach Pastor John Maniatti regarding my concerns about the Community Gospel Church and his leadership methods, He said, "Peter, go forth." I also took this as a sign to go forth into the world as His representative.

3. God had been teaching me through my job that when I go forth in my name and power, I am limited in what I can accomplish; however, when I go forth in the name of God, I can accomplish many things. God was telling me this night that He was sending me forth with the authority to use His name.
4. The Hawaii trip demonstrated to us that God had anointed and empowered us to fight demons, call back the lost, and minister to the deepest needs of people in the world who can hear Him.
5. Last year God told me that in preparation to serve Him, I needed to have more faith in the power of healing—after following his guidance I was healed of high blood pressure, high cholesterol, and a cyst on my wrist.
6. In my prayers to God, I had been telling Him that my life was His to do with as He pleased and that everything I owned—including my home and my family—were ultimately His and to be surrendered to His divine will. Everything! I asked only that He would use me as a dedicated vessel for His work in this world.
7. William said our house was destined to be a mission house, a house of ministry. He frequently told me that I was like Elijah, lifted up on Mount Carmal and empowered by God, that likewise my ministry was to be transformed and blessed by God.
8. Agnes received two scriptures from God while cleaning Williams's room after he left: *Isaiah 55:11* and *Isaiah 46:10-11*. They refer to God's word being disseminated into the world to complete His work, and that He sent a man from a far-away country to give counsel. Likewise, William's counsel brought together and clarified many loose ends in our spiritual lives.
9. God reminded me that in November, 1989 I had prayed for Him to reveal His plan for my life. He told me to read *Zacharia 1:8*, which starts out, "During the night I had a vision." I went to bed excitedly believing I was going to have a dream that night, so convinced that I woke Agnes up and told her about it. But it didn't happen. Now I realize it was prophesying the dream two months later, on January 10, 1990. Praise God!
10. Recently, I was praying for direction concerning the decision to join Jeremiah's ministry. God told me to read *John 15:7*, which says, "If you abide in Me, and My words abide in you, you will ask what you

desire, and it shall be done for you." In my dream I asked the landowner (Lord of the Harvest) if I could be there, and He said yes. This seems to indicate God letting me know the plan for my life includes working with evangelism.
11. My interest to study "In His Name" (see item #3) was initiated by reading in one of the Gospels, "the apostles were continuing to baptize in His name." I believed this to be extremely significant due to the reality of baptizing in the names of Jesus or in the "Name of the Father, Son, and Holy Ghost." I called Agnes to reread it to her once again and it was not there. For several days I tried to find it again and it was not to be found. For some reason God put those words on that page for a while, and then removed them. There is no other explanation.

The Lord of The Harvest is at work in the harvest field and preparing His workers.

United Christian Assembly

During the time we were in Morrisville, Agnes controlled her emotions and actions by reciting and praying, "Create in me a clean heart, Oh God."

Years before, when we were attending Calvary Episcopal Church, we would drive by United Christian Assembly as people were entering for their Sunday service. Agnes noticed how joyful the people looked and had a desire to experience that church someday.

After deciding to leave Community Full Gospel Church in Morrisville, Agnes reminded me that I had promised to bring her to UCA once. But I had recently sworn that I would never again submit to a Christian leader or belong to a church unless it was mine. *But how could I not grant one request from my sweet wife?*

So on October 1, 1990 I drove to UCA and we went inside and sat in a pew. I think it might have been in the front. Agnes looked at the wall on her left and there was a banner with the words, "Create in me a clean heart, Oh God." As she saw it God spoke to her and said, "This is where I want you!" Agnes shared that with me and I knew my previous proclamation was evaporated by the breath of God.

For the next year and a half I sat on my butt in a pew resentfully. I complained to God and he said, "Peter no matter what church you are in, you will be the same with me." The interpretation of that statement: it doesn't matter what church I am in. My relationship is with God and His plans for me are between Him and I. There is no church or person between us.

AMEN!

No more complaining. Time to accept and move forward! But God used UCA to further develop me and Agnes.

At UCA I found new friends and Pastor Duane Hodgeman, who I trusted and found to be submitted to God, and who provided good counsel when I needed it. He was prophetic and God used him to speak into my life.

Prophecy: 3-1-92

by Pastor Duane Hodgeman

Peter, I want to get your attention for a minute because God said something to me about you when I was preaching that I want to share with you. It happened in an interesting way because you were sitting in that seat over there and you had your glasses hanging out of your shirt, and God spoke to me that He was going to begin to allow you to see the heart of God. He's going to let you see His heart towards the people around you.

You've been seeing with your heart, but He's going to give you a greater depth to see with His heart. You're going to be able to see the heart of God in the people around you, to see His heart as it responds to situations in people's lives, and out of that will come healing words. And your words are going to be seasoned with grace. You are going to have a word for those who are weary and for those who are laboring, for those who are downcast and for those who are outcasts of society.

And God's going to help you to see with eyes of understanding, and with eyes of God you're going to be able to see what God sees in the hearts of people. You're going to be able to see their problems. You are going to be able to see their situations and speak His Word with a grace that will deliver and set people free. God's going to give you that heart. He's going to give you His heart, and you are going to see through the eyes of understanding the things of God.

And you are going to be able to speak deliverance and healing into people's lives in the power and anointing of God. You don't have to worry about what people think or gaining their approval, or anything like that.

Just listen to God!

Seek God with all your heart and your mind, and when you see what God sees, RESPOND, because He will give you the Word for he who is weary, and he who needs God's grace.

Amen! Hallelujah! Praise God!

I submit this to you as, "Thus, saith the Lord!" today.

HALLELUJAH! HALLELUJAH! HALLELUJAH!

Prophecy for Pete and Agnes Fiske

Allan Arrowood – United Christian Assembly 11-17-91

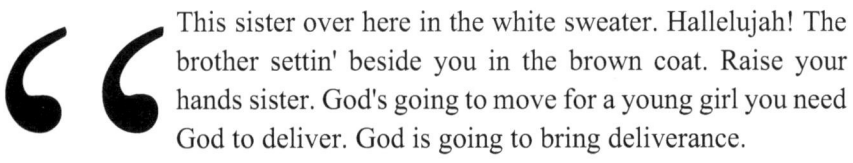

"This sister over here in the white sweater. Hallelujah! The brother settin' beside you in the brown coat. Raise your hands sister. God's going to move for a young girl you need God to deliver. God is going to bring deliverance.

"Hallelujah! Well, Amen! You're going to see the salvation of the Lord.

"Ya'll two married to each other? Hallelujah!

"Raise your hands brother. I just see God really bringing the deliverance. God's breaking some warfare that's been going on in y'alls's life. The enemy has really been trying to drive a wedge in y'alls's life. But God has come to pull the wedge out. God's come to bring a deliverance and to turn y'alls's hearts to each other and to turn your hearts to the Lord greater. And brother you've been through some real battles and the enemy has really fought you, and the enemy has really come against you.

"But God desires to make you two a weapon in the hand of the Lord. As you yield yourself to the Body of Christ and as you yield yourself to the Spirit of God, God is making bare His holy Arm to prove His Self strong in your behalf.

"Hallelujah! Well Glory to God! Hallelujah!"

Note: Allen Arrowood was a Prophet from the hills of South Carolina. He was illiterate, except he could read the Bible. In his vocabulary: Y'all (you singular), Y'alls (you both, plural), Y'alls's (your, plural possessive). A very unique man, loved by many.

Agnes at United Christian Assembly
April, 1992

On April 7, I was at morning prayer and I had a vision of a pair of wide open doors—so open that the doors were not visible. The reason I knew they were doors was that I could see the threshold, frames, and the strip down the middle.

Immediately after that, Duane prayed about God opening doors.

On April 12, during worship, I received the vision of the doors again, and God showed me:

> The doors are open and we have to enter, in faith and trust in Him in all things. And He will hold us up in strength, and He will hold us up in comfort; all we have to do is enter in.

I knew that this was to share with the Assembly. Before I shared it, I could hear God saying, "Agnes! You enter in. Come across the threshold." At that moment I could feel God's love so strongly. I said, "Yes Father!" and I entered. Because of all that God has shown me about faith in the last couple of weeks, and I know I am in a new place in my faith and trust in Him.

Praise God!

> "See, the former things have taken place, and new things I declare; before they spring into being I announce them to you."
>
> *Isaiah 42:9*

The Walk Home

During the evening service at United Christian Assembly, God spoke to me and said, "Peter, walk home." We lived five and a half miles from the church on Poker Hill Rd, a backcountry road that was mostly dirt and gravel. It was a dark, snowy winter night and I wasn't dressed for walking in the cold weather. I had neither hat nor gloves nor boots, and my wife Agnes tried to convince me not to do it because I could get hypothermia, even freeze and die!

But God said walk home, so He outranked Agnes and me. I told her I was going to be obedient to God and that He would take care of me. Upon setting out, my resolve was strong—even my fear of walking in the dark had lifted.

After plodding along for 15 minutes, Agnes and the boys showed up in the car with my hat, gloves and boots as well as a scarf. I never wore scarfs, but she wanted to provide me with all the protection against the cold she could think of.

So far God is taking care of me through my wife, I thought to myself with a smile.

A short while later I was walking in a wooded area where new homes with long driveways had been built back from the road in the woods. I could see light coming from the homes through the trees. The only way I couldn't see the light was if I closed my eyes and turned away, like people in the darkness of sin. They can see the light of Jesus from afar and be drawn through the dark wilderness of their lost souls to repentance or they can harden their hearts and close their eyes as they plunder on in the dark.

Suddenly the quiet was pierced with the sound of a dog outside one of the homes barking at me. As it continued, I became irritated and yelled, "You noisy spirit, be silent in the name of Jesus!"

Immediately the barking ceased.

About halfway home I was passing a field and heard a pair of deer run away through a small beaver pond. I heard them splashing in the water, followed by the loud slap of a beaver's tail on the surface, signaling **DANGER! DANGER!**

I continued my walk on the dark road home and eventually arrived safe, refreshed, and filled with the Holy Spirit.

Warm and cozy in the comfort of our home, I remembered the light shining through the trees in the woods. Then God gave me a vision of the map of Vermont with spots of light sprouting up throughout the state. He let me know that He would establish homes where people would come to hear the Gospel of Jesus Christ, be born again, taught, fed and sent out to share Jesus with the world.

III.

GROWING IN FAITH

The Contractor

In February 1971 I transferred with IBM to a new semiconductor factory in Manassas, Virgina. There were good opportunities for advancement that I wanted to take advantage of. By the time I left in October, 1974 to return to IBM in Vermont, I had received seven promotions in less than ten years. The last two promotions were within management.

We were living in a rented house near downtown Manassas. After two years we bought a building lot in a development 30 miles west on Bull Run Mountain in Haymarket. My father and Agnes' parents helped us with the purchase. We connected with Ridge Homes, a company that would give us a construction loan and shell erect the home, for $100 down payment, followed with monthly payments on the construction loan. They provided all the materials to complete the home along with instructions! I was able to install the electric entrance and copper wiring, the copper plumbing and the electric hot air heating system. I installed the subflooring and preparing to tackle the dry wall installation.

Then an unexpected event quickened our move. We had helped a neighbor and her little girl escape from a very abusive husband who was fresh out of jail. She ended up going back to him and telling him how we helped her. So in retaliation, in the middle of the night, he took his shotgun and blew the side of my car away. My first experience with an ex-convict!

We very quickly moved out of the house in Manassas and moved into our unfinished home on Bull Run Mountain. The home was functional except the water line was not hooked up yet due to a shortage of iron water line for the development. There was a faucet at the end of the waterline on the road that we could hook a long garden hose to and fill a container for drinking water.

So we lived with a plastic portable outhouse in our front yard and no walls or ceilings in the house.

Life was good there surrounded by forest and a neighbor a mile away who let us shower at his place on the weekends. The garden hose in the backyard at home was very cold for showers and we avoided it as much as possible. Our mailbox was also a mile down the road, which was nice—on Saturdays we would send the boys to go get the mail to give us some private time. On the way back they would stop at a neighbor closer to us and the woman would give them cookies and milk. Life on Bull Run Mountain was pleasantly rough.

But as good as the mountain life was, I was very homesick for Vermont. The mountains, valleys, rivers, foliage and weather were calling to me—especially after my grandmother, Matty Fiske, gave me a subscription to *Vermont Life* magazine for Christmas. The pictures in that magazine destroyed any remaining desire I had to live in Virginia.

Bull Run Mountain wasn't Vermont.

❖

When the opportunity to transfer back to IBM in Vermont came we took it. IBM bought our unfinished house with enough profit for us to buy land in Vermont and eventually build another house. My family moved to Vermont in the summer of 1974, but I had to stay in Virginia to complete my assignment there. I remember driving into Vermont and being overwhelmed by the brilliant green landscape. Vermont green is much different than southern green or even New York green. Coming home to Vermont and seeing the mountains was a very emotional experience, bringing tears to my eyes as I drove. French explorer Samuel de Champlain called the Green Mountains of Vermont "Verd Mont" (green mountain) on his 1647 map. He also must have been overwhelmed by the beauty of Verd Mont.

I had been born and grew up in the Champlain Valley, always in sight of the Green Mountain range to the east. As a teenager I wandered through the mountains, exploring, hunting, and fishing in the creeks and streams. I remember my four sons doing the same. My love for the nature of Vermont was longstanding and deep.

After moving the family to a rented house in Milton, I returned to Virginia and lived in a motel until I could move back to Vermont in the fall.

Separating from my wife and children was difficult. At the Burlington Airport, I remember looking at the chain link fence beside the terminal as I was boarding the plane and seeing my son Lee's little fingers clinging to the fence. He was sobbing as he said, "Goodbye Daddy!"

That memory is imbedded in my soul.

By the time October came, I was more than ready to leave Virginia and return to my family in Vermont, the land of my ancestors. My great great great grandfather Stephen Fiske Esquire was the first settler to clear land for farming in Randolph Center. He was a charter member of Randolph and involved in providing the first public stage service from Windsor to Burlington, as approved by the Vermont Legislature in 1795. Today the route to Burlington is 103 miles and can be driven by car on interstates 91 and 89 in 1 hour and 37 minutes. The stage road probably took a bit more time than that, with dirt roads that froze in the winter and then thawed in the spring. No truckloads of gravel to fill in the pits of mud. No diesel powered road graders to smooth out the surface. No cell phone to call AAA or 911 when a stage coach broke down or someone was seriously injured.

❖

A friend from IBM in Manassas who had transferred to Vermont ahead of me had a nice house built by a local contractor and connected me with him. He came to our house in Milton and showed us plans for a 3 bedroom ranch that would be built on a hill with a walkout basement. We got involved in modifying the plans to suit our needs and taste, then were approved for a construction mortgage and the work began.

Work was progressing as planned and we were scheduled to move in by early December, 1976. The contractor gave us the move-in date and we planned accordingly. Arriving at our new home with a loaded moving truck we discovered the house was not ready for us to move in. The heating system, oil-fired hot water, had not been completed, and the basement walls had not been built.

We were in a disaster.

The contractor did not answer his phone. He had obviously abandoned the job. We unloaded the moving truck, and then moved into a two bedroom apartment at the old Essex Motel in Essex Junction.

Agnes' parents Fred and Arlene Dutelle were with us and had to rent a separate room in the motel. Fred was going through cancer treatment in Burlington and needed to be close to the hospital. Arlene needed our support in dealing with what had become a fatal illness.

I had to hire a local plumber to finish the heating system. He told me he had worked with this contractor before and would not work for him unless he was paid in advance.

As stress was building for us, we got a notice that we were being sued by the company that supplied all the materials for the house. Even though we had met all the payments to the builder, he had not paid his supplier.

This was horrible!

We had to go to the lawyer who wrote the construction contract for us and pay him to defend us.

Then Agnes got sick and came down with pneumonia a couple days before Christmas, and it was a difficult Christmas season. I remember getting away for a few hours with my Department Technician from IBM. He had agreed to help do some repairs on my vehicle, and we enjoyed opening a bottle of Canadian Club during the repairs. Somehow the repairs got completed and I made it back to the motel which was about a mile away.

After three years of legal battles, we won by the judge's decision. Had he ruled in favor of the contractor, we would have lost our house. After celebrating victory and enjoying a time of peace, a letter came from our lawyer that the opposing party (a building materials supplier in St Albans) was appealing to the higher Supreme Court. Gloom, despair, and depression settled in at the thought of returning to battle in a higher court.

A short while thereafter, I was skimming through a new Bible, the New English - Oxford Study Edition with Apocrypha, and came to *1 Maccabees 2:62-64*

> Do not fear a wicked man's words, all his success will end in filth and worms. Today he is high in honor, but tomorrow there will be no trace of him, because he will have returned to the dust and all his schemes come to nothing. But you my sons, draw your courage from the law, for by it you will win great glory.

The whole lawsuit was based on lies. We hired a contractor to build our house who promised more than he ever intended to deliver. He abandoned the job without finishing *and* without paying his materials bills to the lumber company. To recover the cost of the materials, the lumber company had sued us both. In court, the lumber company lied, saying we had made verbal agreements to pay them all that was owed. Their lawyer tried to make it look like I had set up the builder—but the judge saw through their deceptiveness and decided in our favor, with the exception of a few hundred dollars.

The builder never showed up for the trial. We also won a countersuit against him for damages and faulty construction. We were not able to collect because, as the lawyer said, he was a "deadbeat" and had nothing of value.

Reading the passage from *Maccabees* inspired me that God was speaking to our situation, giving me the assurance that everything was going to be okay. He was saying, "Don't fear their lies because you are going to win." The verbiage about filth and worms and dust was impressive, but didn't mean much at the time. A year later the higher court denied the other party the right to appeal. Our case was solid and the original judgement was upheld as correct.

Then we read in the paper that the contractor died in a motorcycle accident. All his schemes came to nothing, and he was returned to the dust of the earth. We later learned at the time of his death he'd been chasing his Corvette that was being repossessed for lack of payment. He went off the road on a corner and hit a tree. We were told that before the rescue squad arrived, someone stopped and stole his wallet and gold jewelry.

Years later, his cousin, who also was a contractor, agreed to renovate the kitchen in our house in St Albans. He felt bad about what had been done to us and gave us a good deal on the kitchen. He wanted to somehow restore his family's name.

More recently God reminded me of *1 Maccabees 2:62-64* and what we had endured from 1977-1981. I wondered how that passage was interpreted today. I looked it up in the Good News translation and this is what I found:

> Don't be afraid of the threats of a wicked man. Remember that he will die and all his splendor will end with worms feeding on his decaying body. Today he may be highly honored, but tomorrow he will disappear; his body will return to the earth and his scheming will come to an end. But you, my sons, <u>be strong and courageous in defending the Law</u>, because it is through the Law that you will earn great glory (*1 Maccabees 2:62-64*).

"Defending the Law!" The Word of God!

Sell Your House

In the fall of 1991, I was praying late at night in the yard outside our home on Poker Hill Road, offering myself and everything I own to God for the building up of His kingdom. I was not educated in Seminary or Bible college and had never completed a formal Bible study program. Instead, I'd learned on my own through reading the Bible and applying it to my experience, and my heart's desire was to work for God full time.

While praying, God told me, "Sell your house."

Upon hearing these startling words, I did not run into the house, wake up my wife Agnes and say, "We have to sell the house!" I was a shocked at the idea and did not know how to react. The fear of conflict with my wife, knowing how much she loved our home, was terrifying.

Another night while I was again praying outside in our yard, God told me the same thing, "Sell your house." Again, I did nothing about it. I now understood more than the first time, that if God repeated His request how serious He was. But I was paralyzed, not understanding how to handle God's request.

When God told me to sell the house a third time, His voice was stern and direct, and a **FOR SALE BY OWNER** sign immediately flashed in front of my eyes. I told God, "Lord, You will have to tell Agnes because I can't." This was news she wouldn't likely enjoy hearing, and I knew it would be better coming from God than me.

For the next month God kept prompting me again and again with *Hebrews 11:8:* "By faith Abraham obeyed when he was called to go out to the place which he would receive as an inheritance. And he went out, not knowing where he was going." Though He repeatedly confirmed to me that He wanted me to sell the house, I did not tell Agnes.

Some weeks later, during a Sunday worship service in early December, Agnes suddenly turned to me and said that God had just told her, "Peter is hiding something from you." The same fear of conflict and panic I had been avoiding came flooding back and caused me to tremble. I had asked God to tell her, and He had in a way I did not expect. Now what? The cat was out of the bag, and on the way home I explained what God was doing.

Over the next two months Agnes prayed for confirmation from God, but while God's confirmation came to me steadily, it did not come to her. Then, during a home fellowship meeting, God let her know that she was to fast and pray Friday and Saturday while I was at the Lake Morey Full Gospel Businessmen's retreat.

At the retreat there was a speaker from Texas who told stories about his life as an evangelist. As he spoke, God filled my heart with conviction that it was time to fulfill God's purpose for my life, working in the harvest field. God had given me a message to share with lost and hurting people, and it was time to get off my butt and go to work for Him.

With this revelation I began to tremble uncontrollably and left the meeting to go to my room and calm down. I was so inspired and overwhelmed by God's message that I cried and repented and prayed and rejoiced for an hour. I was so deeply affected and trembling that I could not even hold the utensils to eat dinner, which is quite an anomaly for me. It was embarrassing to sit in the dining room with an empty soup spoon shaking in my hand and unable to use it. So I went back to my room and continued praying and read the Bible.

When I returned home after the retreat, Agnes had been praying and fasting but had not heard from God. The next morning, I attended an early morning prayer meeting at United Christian Assembly, where I shared that I needed to increase my service to God with Pastor Duane and Bernie, a brother in Christ. Bernie responded, "But Pete, you are doing a lot now. I see you at IBM doing Bible studies at lunch. You don't need to burden yourself with trying to do more than you already do." Upon hearing his refutation of God's instruction to me, a holy anger rose up and I became more committed to God's mission for me.

Jesus turned and said to Peter, "Get behind me, Satan! You are a stumbling block to me; you do not have in mind the concerns of God, but merely human concerns" (*Matt 16:23*).

At Sunday worship service Agnes and I received confirmation that we were to kickstart a new phase of our service to the Lord, which also confirmed to Agnes the necessity of selling our home. That was it! We had our orders. The next two days were jarring as we told friends and family about our move. After beginning to doubt again, God reassured me that He had provided for other Believers who took a leap of faith and that He would provide for us. Then I reflected on all that God had already accomplished in our lives and realized there was no excuse for delay.

That's the whole story. Here is my final conclusion: "Fear God and obey His commands, for this is everyone's duty" (*Ecclesiastes 12:13*).

I would walk off a cliff if He told me to.

Wednesday morning God confirmed with Agnes that she was to trust Him and Him alone, which better enabled her to stop listening to the doubting voices of others so we could unify in our preparations to sell the house.

It was a big step for us. We didn't know what was going to happen. We only knew that He told us to do it and had reassured me with *Hebrews 11:8*.

> It was by faith that Abraham obeyed when God called him to leave home and go to another land that God would give him as his inheritance. He went without knowing where he was going. By an act of faith, Abraham said yes to God's call to travel to an unknown place that would become his home.

We were excited about the upcoming adventure God had for us. Others were fearful for us to move forward without seeing the plan and not knowing what would happen. But not us! When I reflected on our lives, I saw the work He had been accomplishing through us for years. In pursuing His mission for us, I saw God had always provided and been in complete control. When we were obedient to Him, living the vision He had for our lives, we were anointed, provided for and blessed all the way.

I didn't know what would become of us when the house sold, but I was confident that God was in control, had a purpose and would take care of us. Many people thought we were crazy and being misled because we lacked a clear vision of what God was doing. They said God would have given us a vision of His plan. I told them God had already done enough with our lives to reassure me that we were safely in His hands.

My best guess was that God was leading us out of debt and we would end up with a more affordable and paid-for home in a community where He could use us to minister to others.

I kiddingly said to Agnes, "We should get enough money from the house to buy a good-sized crusade tent. We'll hit the sawdust trail."

She didn't laugh.

Burn My House Down

"But Jesus said, 'No one, having put his hand to the plow, and looking back, is fit for the Kingdom of God.'"

Luke 9:62

As of February 2, 1993 we had done nothing to sell our house. But this was our home! The Fiske clan homestead where we raised our sons, a small herd of milk goats, sheep, pigs, ducks and rabbits. The home where we tended vegetable gardens, reached the crisis that brought us to the Lord, and became born again!—then spent 3 years in a court battle with the builder who failed to complete the house as contracted and did not pay his material bills.

Since this particular day was a Sunday, we made our way to the United Christian Assembly in Underhill Flats. While worshipping, I was standing on a large floor grate. When the furnace came on hot air blew up all around me. The furnace must have been old because a whiff of oil smoke hit my nostrils.

Immediately, God spoke very sternly and said, "Peter, if you don't sell your house, I will sell it to your fire insurance company." As soon as I heard those words, the fire alarm at the fire station a ¼ mile up the street blasted loudly. I could hear the firemen rushing to the station with their vehicle sirens in unison with the loud alarm from the station.

Fear came over me as I thought, "He is burning my house down without giving me a chance. God don't burn my house down."

In my Christian life so far God had been a gentle, loving Father who saved me, restored my marriage and family, and protected us all. My "Fear of the Lord" which now surged through my veins was soon relieved as I heard the fire truck sirens screaming past the church going south—our house was to the north.

When the service was over, we went straight to Jerihill Hardware Store in Jericho and bought a **FOR SALE BY OWNER** sign. When we got home, I posted it at the bottom of our driveway. Agnes' 46th birthday had been the previous day. Happy Birthday Agnes!

I learned that God wants obedience.

And He gets what He wants.

> "And now, Israel, what does the Lord your God require of you, but to fear the Lord your God, to walk in all His ways and to love Him, to serve the Lord your God with all your heart and with all your soul."
>
> *Deuteronomy 10:12*

Kairos

The first attempt to organize a Kairos weekend involved a partnership between Protestants and the Catholic Diocese of Vermont, but it fell apart when the Catholic Bishop would not agree to it. A year later the partnership was approved, the training sessions began, and, in March of 1992, the first Kairos weekend took place.

I was excited by the opportunity to speak about God to a group of inmates. However, when the speaking assignments were handed out, I was tasked with the first talk which did not mention God at all.

Eeek!

My assignment was to provide cookies and coffee to the tables where inmates and other team members were sitting and sharing. I'd been given the worst, most boring assignment of all, but I deserved it because I had declared I would help once but was unwilling to continue with prison ministry after that weekend. By this point, I had already turned down requests to participate in prison ministry with Glenn and Ellie Martin.

The opening session of the weekend was Thursday night in the gymnasium of North West State Correctional Facility (NWSCF). We were all required to "sponsor" one inmate, which meant to befriend the person for the duration of the weekend. As inmates filed into the gym, their names were called out and the sponsor introduced themself. The inmate I was assigned to sponsor was a man named John Kane. When he walked into the gym and his name was called, I looked up and saw the scariest, meanest man I had ever encountered. Fear poured through me and I worried that I might not make it out alive from the weekend.

John Kane was 6 feet tall, his skin a tanned bronze, and had a physique resembling a steel railroad spike. He sported an unruly afro and wore a

Satanic-looking T-shirt that made me cringe. "God please protect me," I prayed fervently. "But if you led me here to be a martyr for your Kingdom, your will be done."

Regardless of my trepidation, I walked over to John, introduced myself and shook his hand. My fear began to subside when he spoke in a friendly tone and we began to share about ourselves. John was an expert guitar player and told me he was studying new music theories—which sounded very impressive to me, being a person who knows as much about music theory as I do astrophysics. Zilch!

The evening program was good and I gave my "Godless" talk, during which I wasn't allowed to mention God, Jesus or the Holy Spirit. But, it turns out, God had it all under control for his own purposes.

By the next day I found myself praying for John and other inmates as my heart filled with compassion and love for them.

What was happening to me? The man who had refused the call to prison ministry so many times ... Was the prison booby trapped to capture me?? Why was I feeling things I didn't want to feel?

Eventually, God removed those thoughts from my mind and turned me around, causing me to repent without even knowing it. By the end of the weekend I had made friends with several of the inmates and promised to come back to meet with them individually for one-on-one sessions. During this time I was allowed to come to the prison anytime and meet individually with inmates. I soon became a regular visitor at NWSCF, meeting one on one with several inmates.

One of the first inmates I met with was Dave B. He asked me to be a support person for him after he was released. I asked, "What's a support person?"

He said, "Someone to be a friend and help in the transition from prison back to society." When I asked him what his crime was, he said, "I perpetrated against my daughter."

Wow! He perpetrated? It sounded clinical, but I had no idea what that meant. I guessed that made him a "perp." Regardless, I agreed to be a support person for him.

Later, I would learn the details of his crime as I became more involved with him and eventually one of his daughters.

Church Service

In September 1992, after a few months of meeting one on one with individuals, I decided to visit the Sunday evening church service run by Denis Chevalier, an elder at the Church of The Rock in St. Albans. However, this was no normal church, it was held at the local St. Albans prison, officially known as the Northwest State Correctional Facility (NWSCF), where I was patted down by correctional facility security guards before being admitted. Working alongside Denis were Pat Hoadley, a Truck Driver, and Rev Ed Hackett, a Methodist Pastor who would preach once a month as well as Cindy Weed, who brought her guitar to provide worship music.

A few days after the Kairos weekend, just a week or so after my first visit to the Sunday evening church service at NWSCF, I received a call from Denis who had been injured in a sports accident. His Achilles tendon was broken and he would be out of action for a couple months. He had no one to run the Sunday Church service, so I told him, "I'll get a couple guys and run it for you until you come back." But on Sunday I didn't have a couple guys, so my wife Agnes and I went to the prison and led the service. Cindy Weed was there with her guitar for worship time. I provided the sermon, which I had worked on for 20 hours. (Fortunately, over time my sermons became better and took less time to develop!)

Truthfully, I had no idea how to run a prison church service, but God had placed others there with experience who assisted me and helped me to learn. Among the inmates were two mature Christians who provided encouragement and were mentors for other inmates. Fellowshipping with these inmates who were seeking God became the highlight of our lives.

As we shared our prison ministry experience at United Christian Assembly one of the men in the congregation decided he wanted to help us. He seemed very sincere and knew the Bible very well. However, when he came with us he became embroiled in a theological debate with one of the inmates. The man was very intense in explaining his view of Biblical principles, which enraged the inmate, who walked out of the service and threatened to kill the man the next time he came—so I made sure the inmate did not return to the service until he met with me and repented. I also told the man from UCA he could not come back to NWSCF. This experience made me realize we had to be very careful in who we chose to volunteer with us.

A short while into the ministry God let me know that it was actually a Church inside the prison. Eventually, our name became The Church At Prison. I had been inspired by the preaching of Pastor Vince Circello who said that we were all one Church, one Body under the Lordship of Jesus Christ, and one day we would refer to "The Church in Underhill" and "The Church in Burlington" rather than to churches separated by denominations.

After two months Denis had healed and was able to come back to the Sunday night service. As he was being checked in he put his VT DOC Badge on and noticed that we were beyond the expiration date. Considering what to do about this, God spoke to him and said, "Your time here has expired."

So Denis came into the service and told us he was not coming back, that he would meet with the Board at Church of The Rock, a few individuals who had invested their time and talent in the ministry, and recommend the ministry be turned over to us. They agreed and he informed us that, as of December 1992, the prison ministry was our responsibility.

WOW!

The next Sunday we went into prison for the church service and informed the inmates of the decision. Roger "Mike" Hammond and Wayne Delisle, both senior Christian inmates, gathered everyone around us. There we were surrounded by murderers, sex offenders, thieves, drug dealers, violent offenders, all the people God gave me love for. They all joined in laying on of hands and prayed with Mike as he led the prayer, accepting me as their new pastor. This was our commissioning and credentialing by God. Other commissionings, licensings and ordinations have followed in the years since that day, but this event was the most precious and meaningful one.

I am reminded of the men of Judah going to Hebron and anointing David as their King, in *2 Samuel 2:4*. Both Mike and Wayne have passed away in recent years; however, they remain my 'Forever" brothers in Christ. A few months later I was licensed as a Minister of The Gospel of Jesus Christ. Some of the counseling I was involved in at the prison DOC required me to be credentialed.

On May 16 Pastor Duane filled in for us at the Sunday night church service at prison. The following morning I met with Pastor Duane and after praying together he looked at me intently and said, "Peter, I saw the need there. God needs to release you from IBM so you can go full time."

Although Pastor Duane was younger than me, he was like a spiritual father. God was speaking to me through him.

So I listened.

A Walk In The Dark

On May 18, 1993 I woke up early and went to work. I arrived at my IBM office at 5:30 a.m. and opened an old, well-worn Bible that I used for Bible study during lunch. Normally, I would start to work when I arrived, but this morning I had a desire to read God's Word first.

As I put the Bible on my desk, it fell open to *Isaiah* and I began to read *Chapter 42*. When I arrived at *Verse 5,* my heart began to pound as I knew God was speaking to me:

> Thus says God the Lord, Who created the heavens, and stretched them out; Who spread forth the earth, and that which comes from it; Who gives breath to the people on it, and spirit to those who walk upon it: "I, the Lord, have called you in righteousness, and will hold your hand, I will keep you, and give you as a covenant to the people, As a light to the Gentiles, To open blind eyes, To bring out prisoners from the prison, Those who sit in darkness from the prison house. I am the Lord: that is My name, and My Glory will I not give to another, nor my praise to graven images. Behold, the former things have come to pass, and new things I declare: Before they spring forth I tell you of them (*Isaiah 42:5-9).*

God was telling me it was time to leave IBM and transition to full-time Prison Ministry. The moment had come. I had prayed for 14 years about offering my life entirely to serve God, and that morning the answer arrived.

As if on cue from God, that day IBM announced a retirement option that fit my need. I would leave IBM after 28 years, using a 2-year pre-retirement leave of absence, with one year's salary. My pension would begin in two years. Although it was a good long-term option, it still didn't account for the next two years.

When I got home after work I shared the scripture with Agnes and told her of the retirement offering. She was excited and relieved to know God's plan for us. We both agreed that accepting the retirement offering was God's will for our lives. Until then we were not sure how selling the house fit into our future. The FOR SALE BY OWNER sign had been up for 16 months, with no buyer interest. God had told us to do it. God told me that He was sending me into full-time prison ministry. But the house was not selling and I was retiring!

I met with Pastor Duane the next morning on my way to work and told him I was going to retire. He advised me to work out a financial plan that would keep us going for a year. This would give me time to build up a support base that would provide what we needed to live on and to operate the ministry.

I informed my IBM manager that I was going to retire and in a few days the management team produced a retirement plan. I signed the plan and it was done. June 30 would be my last day. July 1, 1993 would be my first day as an IBM retiree and a full-time Prison Pastor!

That evening I worked on the financial plan, but the best I could do was make the money we had last about 6 months—and we needed more than that. In fact, my plan was overly-optimistic; in reality, the money would not likely last 6 months.

Fear descended on me that night, and I could no longer work on the plan so I went to bed where Agnes was already asleep. As I lay there praying, the Lord spoke to me: "Peter! Get up and come out with Me." He was inviting me to go outside and pray. So I went out on the deck and looked up into a beautiful night sky that was blazing with stars.

As I was praying *and complaining* to Him about money, He again spoke to me. "Take a walk in the dark. Go to the end of the driveway and back." That was tough. I have been afraid of the dark ever since I was a little child.

When I was 5 and we lived in Weybridge, I would go upstairs to where we had a chemical toilet, a big tank with a seat on it. It was located in a small room that had a doorway and stairs up to the attic, a scary place filled with tigers and lions. At such times, I would talk to the tiger in the attic and tell him, "Don't come out yet, Mr. Tiger. You can't come out yet." All the way back down stairs, I would say, "You can't come out yet." When I got to the bottom of the stairs I would yell, "OK! You can come out now, Mr. Tiger."

Then I slammed the door in his face.

When I was 7 or 8 and we lived in Middlebury, my father let me go to the movies one night to see *Frankenstein*. I spent the better part of the next hour and a half hiding behind the seat in front of me, shaking with fear. Afterwards, I had the arduous task of walking a mile down dark streets to our house—a feat of bravery I accomplished by keeping to the middle of the road, as far as possible from the bushes and trees on the sides of the street.

Needless to say, I'd had a profound fear of the dark since childhood. So when the Lord gave me a direct command that night, it posed an awesome challenge. As I walked down the driveway into the darkness I felt every hair on my body stand up stiff in apprehension of the unknown. I felt the monster's claws reach out to grab me. I saw strange shadows move and jump all around.

I began to pray loudly, rebuking the demon spirits. Somehow I made it to the end of the driveway (a mere tenth of a mile), then turned around and started back. As I got closer to the house and became hopeful that I might live through the experience, my fear of the dark lifted. And as I started up the steps to the deck, I realized I was no longer afraid of the financial challenge either.

God said, "Peter, I took care of your fear of the dark. I will take care of the money. Do not fear!"

Then I remembered *Isaiah 42:6-7*.

> I, the Lord, have called you in righteousness; I will take hold of your hand. I will keep you and will make you to be a covenant for the people and a light for the Gentiles, to open eyes that are blind, to free captives from prison and to release from the dungeon those who sit in darkness.

That's what He did. He held my hand and walked me through the darkness and delivered me from my dungeon of fear.

Agnes also prayed and God gave her *Ruth 3:11*: "And now, my daughter, do not fear. I will do for you all that you request, for all the people of my town know that you are a virtuous woman."

Agnes recorded in her journal: "My portion for ministry. A continuation of *Isaiah 42:6-7* that God gave to Peter."

God also gave her *Ruth 2:12*: "The Lord repay your work, and a full reward be given you by the Lord God of Israel, under whose wings you have come for refuge."

Agnes and I realized this was God's Kairos time to launch us into a full-time ministry that had been my desire for many years. Together we walked through the dark towards God's light.

"Delight yourself also in the Lord, And He shall give you the desires of your heart."

Psalm 37:4

The House Sale

On July 22, 1993 we realized we could no longer continue to try to sell our house on our own. We needed to list it with a realtor, put our effort into the ministry, and let God worry about the details.
Give Up, Let God!
On July 28, the first couple that came to look at it signed a contract to buy it. Two days later we celebrated my 49th birthday. Memories of our life on Poker Hill Road were coming to an end. We finished raising our sons in that home. We saw them leave for college, military service, marriage and foreign missions. We traveled to colleges in Vermont and Maine. We went to weddings in Vermont, Hawaii and The Dominican Republic.

Agnes was always fearful of life after children and the empty nest. But the empty nest was being sold and we had to find another. Little did we know that the new nest would be filled with a wide spectrum of visitors, from bishops to criminals, and sons and their wives and children.

Life would not be empty.

On August 2 we began the search for a home and the first house we looked at was everything we had desired. On August 5 we signed a contract to buy it.

Once we got out of God's way, He was quick and efficient.

The people buying our house were Christians. Our Real estate agent was a Christian. The bank appraiser was a Christian, and the Civil engineer that resolved a problem with a missing state permit was a Christian. Even the real estate agent that we had in St. Albans was a Christian. Nearly everyone involved in the sale of our home was a Christian, and the others heard our testimony of what God was doing in our lives.

On September 16, we moved out of the Underhill home and spent a week living with Bill and Marion Eastman, who had been Christian friends for several years. On the day we moved out of the Underhill home, we had many Christian friends help us load the trucks. Our home fellowship from United Christian Assembly (now renamed Catalyst on Raceway) met at our house that night and helped clean up.

On September 22, 1993 we closed on both houses. The new owners were Charles and Susan Skelly, and it was Susan's birthday. They were not able to have children so they had cats. One year later, on September 22, 1994, Susan gave birth to their first child.

Happy birthday and Praise God!

With the snap of His fingers God can accomplish many things at once. Our God is an awesome God.

By Saturday, September 26 we finally moved in to our new home on North Main Street in St Albans. Praise God! God put together a plan for us and used His people to make it happen. He is faithful to that which He promises, for the sake of His name, and, at times, in spite of us.

OUR GOD IS AN AWESOME GOD!

Christmas, 1993

"I, the Lord, have called You in righteousness, And will hold Your hand; I will keep You and give You as a covenant to the people, As a light to the Gentiles, To open blind eyes, To bring out prisoners from the prison, Those who sit in darkness from the prison house."

Isaiah 42:6-7

The Underhill house sold for $105,000, and we bought a house on Main Street in St. Albans for $64,000, four miles from the prison. With selling high and buying low, we were introduced to capital gains tax. WOW! But it didn't matter because we were following God's directions.

By November we were out of money.

Since I had left IBM on a pre-retirement leave of absence, I wouldn't be getting a pension check until July, 1995. It felt like a hopeless situation calling for desperate action. We decided to cash in our gold jewelry. I had a gold ring someone had given me as a gift, and Agnes had some miscellaneous gold jewelry. Altogether we made enough to live on for another month. But a short while later, heading into the Christmas season of 1993, the bank account was empty.

Meanwhile, Beryl Martinique, an elderly friend, was reviewing her finances for the year and realized that she was short in her tithing to the Lord. As she pondered where to send a check, the doorbell rang. It was the mailman with mail she needed to sign for. But, lo and behold, in the pile of envelopes he delivered she found one of our first newsletters.

POW!

The <u>Dunamis</u> power of God made it obvious that the check needed to go to the Fiske's in St Albans. It was enough to get us into the new year.

Checks from other donors soon followed hers. One of the first was a check from Jericho Congregational Church. I called and asked what the check was for. They said, "Didn't you know? You are on our missions." I thought, "What is missions?" They told me missions committees decide where a church will send donations, and they had recognized The Church At Prison as a ministry worthy of donations.

I remembered that God had spoken to me through *Isaiah 42:6*: "I will hold Your hand; I will keep You." From the moment I read this passage and followed Him into ministry, God had guided and supported me. It was a promise He had kept for 31 years. He provided my keep of essentials for living because I was in the keep of The Shepherd.

God called upon me to serve as a prison and aftercare minister and promised to "take me by the hand and keep me." I have remained in His possession, and He has guided me in the course He set for me.

Happy New Year, 1994

Agnes' first journal entry after moving to St Albans and full time ministry:

January 1, 1994 Saturday.

"Now faith is the substance of things hoped for, the evidence of things not seen" (*Hebrews 11:1*).

If only I had kept the daily journal of happenings till now. What a time of love, blessings and changes, miracles, joys, tears, pain—everything, but most of all God's love, direction, peace, joy and mighty miracles. We sold our house in September to a born again, spirit-filled couple, and bought a house at 230 N Main St. in St. Albans.

A very bittersweet time. Joy and peace in doing God's will and yet the pain of separating from friends and the home we so much loved. Well home has been here since October and what an adjustment—country to city, friends all long distance, Peter's office at home, meeting new people. What a mighty work God is doing in the hearts of prisoners through my beloved husband. Our relationship has been through adjustments, many ups and downs. Sometimes I forget that it's Satan coming to rob and steal, and really think that Peter has ceased to care and he forgets, and ministry becomes all-consuming and we come back around. But we have a much better grasp on it now.

We are learning much! Praise God for his grace and mercy. Father, I love you and I yearn to be closer and closer to you.

Hold me father as a child. Teach me and show me your ways and will for me. Draw into deeper relationship, myself, the husband of my youth and you, Father. Make me a better helpmate, Oh Lord!

Help me Lord to be a woman of wisdom and impart that to my children. Most of all, Lord, create in me a pure heart so I may know you more and love you more.

Praise you Lord.

Panic and Repent

"And Peter answered Him and said, 'Lord, if it is You, command me to come to You on the water.' So He said, 'Come.' And when Peter had come down out of the boat, he walked on the water to go to Jesus. But when he saw that the wind *was* boisterous, he was afraid; and beginning to sink he cried out, saying, 'Lord, save me!' And immediately Jesus stretched out *His* hand and caught him, and said to him, 'O you of little faith, why did you doubt?'"

Mathew 14:28-31

After the first few months of our ministry, the funds hit another low point. We were not able to pay all our bills, and they were starting to pile up at the end of the month. Succumbing to old habits, I allowed fear to creep in and began to panic about our ability to support ourselves on donations alone. I started thinking about going to our bank to get a loan that would help us manage until my pension kicked in another year. We used to have revolving credit with our bank, before retirement, and relied on it frequently.

Going into the ministry, we had no debt and had budgeted our lifestyle so that living expenses were very low. It was 1994, and Agnes and I were surviving on $1500 a month, with no extra funds to draw from in our bank account, no "wiggle room" for emergencies. Some months our income was even lower, and this time I allowed fear to take control.

My plan was to go to the bank the next day and ask for a loan, but I felt guilty. I was troubled and couldn't sleep. Around midnight I went into the living room, kneeled and repented to God, asking Him to forgive me for not putting my faith in Him and His promises.

Peace came to me, and I was able to return to bed and sleep.

The next morning I went to the post office to retrieve the mail and found a letter from our friend Beryl. Inside was a note saying, "Don't thank me for this one. God told me to send it." Alongside the note was a check for $1,000.

Praise God. He knew I would reach a crisis, repent and go to the post office the next day!

Our God is an AWESOME God.

In *Isaiah 42:6* God told me "I will keep you"! I was being "kept."

The Rose

by Agnes Fiske

Peter and I were invited to the wedding of a very special young couple from our Church, the United Christian Assembly of Jericho. The wedding was Sunday, December 14th at 5 p.m., and we were unable to attend because no one was available to fill in for us at the Sunday Evening Church Service at Northwest State Correctional Facility.

I was very disappointed to say the least.

The next morning, driving on Raceway Road to the Church, I saw Mt. Mansfield with fresh snow on it, alongside all the surrounding landscape in its white splendor. All of a sudden the tears started flowing from my eyes, and I realized they were coming from a deep longing in my heart to move back to Underhill, where I could be more active in the life of the Church body and close to most of my dearest friends.

I wept as the pain became almost too much to bear. Drawing closer to the Church, I asked God to take that longing from me.

As I opened the car door in the Church parking lot, I looked down to find a red rose on the snow-covered ground. I picked it up and studied it, noticing that it was completely frozen and absolutely perfect. Even the ice crystals on it were a sight to behold!

This rose had been through high winds, a snowstorm, people walking and cars driving through the parking lot, and yet it was untouched. I knew that the rose was from the wedding, and that I had been blessed!

I ran in and shared it with Sandy, our Church Secretary. She told me that she had just walked through the parking lot and had not seen the rose. I knew then that it was meant for me, and I also knew that there was more to come from this treasure.

The next morning I was at the St. Cyr's home and shared what happened with Diane (mother of the groom) and another Christian sister. Of course, we all thought it was a grand experience, one that only God could arrange!

We had gathered to pray, and as we began to praise and worship the Lord, He revealed to me that I could return to living in Underhill and be His, but be in a frozen state like the rose I had found, or I could remain in St. Albans and be a rose that is blooming.

I knew that God allowed me to find that rose to show me that living in St. Albans was exactly where He wanted me to be.

The Snow Geese

In November, Agnes and I took a day trip to Plattsburg, NY on our day off. Driving south on Rte. 9, we passed a freshly harvested corn field. The barren ground was dotted thickly with beautiful white snow geese—there must have been 800 of them.

I turned the car around and drove back to park on the side of the road so we could take in this vision of splendor. The snow geese were all facing south into the wind as if awaiting the right moment to rise up and take flight.

"But those who wait on the Lord shall renew their strength; they shall mount up with wings like eagles, they shall run and not be weary, they shall walk and not faint."

Isaiah 40:31

At times, a small group would lift into the air briefly and move to another part of the field where they would settle down and again face into the wind. I had the feeling that God was showing us something, but I wasn't sure what.

It seemed late in the season to be seeing snow geese. Canadian geese had already migrated south.

Days later, I was remembering the snow geese and God showed me that they were like His people that had submitted to the Holy Spirit. They were waiting on the Lord and facing into the wind of the Holy Spirit as it moved over the land, waiting for the precise time when the Spirit would say, "Come fly with me."

In December, we returned to Plattsburg on an overnight trip for R&R and to finish up some Christmas shopping. I had thanked the Lord for the message from the snow geese in November and was wondering if they would still be there this late in December. If they were, I knew it was God holding them there for another message.

Once again, driving south on Rte. 9 we saw a large group of these celestial creatures flying in formation. The whole group was composed of a few smaller groups all in their V formations. No one bird or group was the leader of the whole flock. Rather, they were all flying together in their separate groups, yet moving as a portion of the whole flock.

God was showing me that His people were moving on the wind of the Holy Spirit, following the lead of the Spirit rather than any single bird or group.

Later that night, as we ate supper at a restaurant on the lake shore, we saw small flocks of snow geese coming from different directions and landing on the water for the night. Many groups came and formed a much larger group that floated as one on the water. God was showing us that His people come together for rest and refreshment, like Agnes and I were doing on that trip.

God's message through the snow geese led me to believe that we are part of a greater migration of the Holy Spirit in this area. He is raising up many different groups and individuals to do His work. In following Him, they come together for nourishment, refreshment, rest, and work.

Clearly, God is the leader and we are riding on the Wind of His Spirit.

The Master

On my second sleepless night recovering from an illness, I lay in bed troubled by all the frustrating situations in my life. *Was the enemy keeping me awake? Or was God keeping me awake to share the midnight solitude and darkness with Him?* Either way, I wasn't going to sleep, and the right thing to do was to commune with God. It seemed easy, in the state I was in, to get intensely intimate with Him. As I talked to Him, He delivered my mind from the tormenting thoughts.

Then He began to teach me about the Master's Tools. He showed me how many times people thank and praise Agnes and I for the ministry we do. Even though we give the glory to Him, others often give the glory to us—and we permit this because it feels good. He reminded me of his instruction in *Isaiah 42:8*: "I am the Lord, that is My name; and My Glory I will not give to another, nor My Praise to graven images."

Then He took me back to July 1, 1993—the day after I left IBM to pursue God's calling. The next day Agnes and I hit the road for a 3-day vacation to Maine as a brief reprieve and rejuvenation before beginning our full-time ministry. Much to our chagrin, somewhere on Vt. Rte. 302, just outside of Barre, our pickup truck began to die. With each obnoxious groan of the engine, the rocky shore at Two Light Point in Cape Elizabeth grew farther and farther away. Maybe we would never get there, never sit on the rocks with our clamburgers and watch the tide come in. Maybe we would never see that place again...or so my apprehensive thoughts taunted me.

We limped back to the Chevy dealer in Barre, and after waiting an hour the verdict was in: the electric fuel pump was in need of replacement. The pump demon had returned to haunt me again!

Six months earlier I had spent $200 to have a mechanic fix what he said was a bad fuel-sending unit. Three miles down the road the vehicle broke down again. I had gone to him because his hourly rate was half of what other mechanics charged and because he was only a mile from our house. Frustrated, I had called Bill Clark's Interstate Sunoco in Williston. Bill is a Master Mechanic. He could fix anything and seemed to know everything about vehicles, including their design weaknesses.

The Master can fix it!

Our truck ended up at Clark's where one of Bill's mechanics took it apart, only to discover it was not the fuel-sending unit, it was the pump. In fact, the previous mechanic had done some damage. Under the expert, caring eye of Bill Clark the problem had been fixed at a cheaper cost than what the other mechanic had charged. When you know what you are doing, you can do something in a lot less time. $40 an hour for 1 hour is cheaper than $25 an hour for 6 hours.

But that was six months ago and here we were broke down again, this time in Barre, and Bill's pump had broke. Worse still, the dealer wanted all our vacation money to fix it. Not willing to sacrifice our needed recuperation time, I made haste to a telephone and called Bill Clark's Interstate Sunoco. Bill answered and said, "Bring it here if you can."

We said goodbye to the man who wanted our vacation money and went back to the master. At Bill's, the master's eyes watched as his mechanic took apart the gas tank and removed the broken part. I don't know what kind of warranty he originally gave me on the part, but I believe it had been more than 6 months since he fixed it. He was able to get another replacement part right away and had it repaired in about an hour and a half. (Thank you, Lord!)

"No charge," said the master. We thanked him and told him what we were doing with our lives. Then we set out on the road more confident that we would enjoy our clamburgers on the rocky shore in Maine.

Bill has been very good to us over the years. What he does, he does correctly, with no wasted time. Whenever I buy a vehicle, I take it to the master first. He checks it carefully and advises me as to what is wrong and the cost to fix it. He has saved me thousands of dollars by avoiding bad deals. Of all the cars he has inspected for me, I think he has only charged me $14.

Everyone in the business knows the master. "He's honest," they say. He hires top rate mechanics and pays them well. He also has good tools. I used to buy the cheap ones that are labeled "Made in Taiwan" until I learned that they break in the middle of a job when your vehicle is disabled and you are 20 miles from an auto parts store. The master is too smart to invest in cheap tools—which is why he's the master.

In my recollection of my times with the master, God reminded me that when Mechanic Bill Clark heals my broken vehicle I don't run over and kiss his half-inch drive socket in thanksgiving. I don't shake the handle of the lift that picks up the vehicle and puts it back down again. I shake the hand of the master mechanic.

In the same way, God showed me that I am His tool. My mission and purpose is to lead people to Him, not to myself. Recalling this made me realize that instead of permitting praise and glory to come to Agnes and myself, we should lead people to the Master and teach them to give it to Him. Likewise, when someone ministers to us effectively, we need to thank God and give Him praise.

If we shower the minister with praise and glory that belongs to God, we are worshiping a tool instead of God. That is Sin. We may also be setting up that tool of God for trouble—so we need to keep our focus on God.

"My Glory I will not give to another, nor My Praise to graven images."

The Car

"I, the LORD, have called You in righteousness, and will hold Your hand; I will keep You."

Isaiah 42:6a

I was in need of a car, but had no money to buy one, and with our meager income by donations, I was unable to finance. Seemingly in an unresolvable dilemma, out of the blue I received a call from Al Coutes, a homeless man I knew from the Burlington Emergency Shelter. He was a former drug addict who was mentally challenged, but a solid Christian, and a very nice man.

I could barely believe it, Al, a homeless man, had a car to give me.

A few years earlier I had been on staff at the shelter on Friday nights, checking people in and using a breathalyzer to sort out those under the influence. Al was living there. One night my son Lee was helping me, and Al came in out of the cold with no coat on, shivering. Lee took off his nice leather, fleece-lined jacket and gave it to him. Al very much appreciated that warm jacket.

Since that time, Al had worked, saved his money, and obtained his driver's license after a 30-year hiatus. He bought a nice used Chevy Z24 Cavalier. It was a hot rod and the first time he drove it, he ran it into a tree. The car was towed to McRea's Salvage Yard in St. Albans and his plan was to have it repaired. The repair parts were ordered and ready, but the owner of the salvage yard refused to repair the car because he knew that Al was unable to drive properly and would end up getting in another accident, and maybe get killed.

Al ended up giving me the car, and enough cash along with the parts to repair it. In a short time, I had sporty transportation. Awesome! God used a homeless man living in a homeless shelter to provide what I needed.

The car served me well until one day I was driving to meet a client in Essex Junction at the Lincoln Inn for breakfast. As I turned into the parking lot I was broadsided by an off-duty policeman. The force of the impact apparently knocked me unconscious for a few seconds. I opened my eyes and my car was in the parking lot and someone was opening my door.

But the accident was my fault. A man in a red pickup had stopped and signaled me with what I thought was a sign it was safe to navigate through three lanes of oncoming traffic. It turns out I misinterpreted the sign!

The policeman was a Christian and walked home to get his wife's car, and then came back and drove me to Burlington to get a rental. The man in the pickup apologized to me and turned out to be a Christian also. I had a good conversation with him, and he ended up becoming a donor, then, a few years later, a missionary overseas.

My client was a no-show.

At some point I called Agnes to let her know about the accident. I became emotional as I described it and started sobbing. So I ended the call abruptly—the wrong thing to do. Agnes panicked and called our pastor to go to the Lincoln Inn to rescue me. Of course, I wasn't there. I was enjoying a free ride to Burlington to get the rental car and a good conversation with the policeman. As it turned out, the insurance from the accident paid the cost for a replacement car, so what Al did still provided my need for a car, despite the trauma of the accident.

Cell phones had not come into use then. Nowadays, we can be in touch with someone and know what's happening almost instantly. Poor Agnes never knew what happened after the accident until I showed up at home with a rental car. I am sure she called the hospital to see if I was there. Maybe she called the Essex Police to see if they could tell her what happened to me after the accident. But God knew what was happening. God also heard Agnes praying in desperation and brought her peace.

I have learned that God uses imperfect people to accomplish His purposes. He cleans up the messes we make, corrects our errors, provides what we need when we can't, and brings peace when there is turmoil.

> "And we know that all things work together for good to those who love God, to those who are the called according to His purpose."
>
> *Romans 8:28*

He is with me always and takes my hand to guide me when I don't know where to go or what to do. He provides my keep, to sustain me in serving His purposes. He keeps His promises. He is faithful to His contract with me.

He is my Father!

> "I, the LORD, have called You in righteousness, And will hold Your hand; I will keep You and give You as a covenant to the people, As a light to the Gentiles."
>
> *Isaiah 42:6-9*

Sweet Perfume

Last night during our Fellowship meeting in the prison a man appeared to be getting tormented demonically. After the meeting he asked for prayer and I prayed on him with two brothers, Fred and Ron, who are trained in deliverance. As we began to pray the demon growled, spoke in unholy tongues, and then became quiet. As we prayed he went down, slain in the Spirit, and we continued until there was peace and he was able to get up again. He was greatly relieved and smiled as he wiped the sweat off his face.

This same brother had manifested in a similar fashion over a year ago. I had just been through a deliverance training seminar given by Fred Grewe in preparation for Randy Clark speaking at Killington '97. He is the only one that has ever manifested like this. Any other deliverance we have done in prison has been quiet and without any of the physical manifestations. We are thankful for that since there is no privacy in prison.

I was feeling high on the Holy Spirit during the Fellowship meeting until we were faced with the need for deliverance. Listening to the demon speaking through the man made me feel like I had rolled in dirt and got filthy. I was thinking, "What a horrible ending to a wonderful meeting!" Yuk!

As we were walking out of the dining room to leave for the night, we went through the door into the main hallway and could smell something sweet. It became stronger as we walked, until Agnes said, "Is that perfume? I smell perfume!"

I recognized the smell and said, "That's anointing oil. Somehow it must have broken inside my briefcase. The deliverance was so powerful that it burst my oil vials. What a mess that will be. I'll have to leave my briefcase outdoors for a week to air out. All the skunks in St. Albans will come running to it. Ha Ha!"

The scent became more pungent as we walked down the hall. I was embarrassed it was coming from my briefcase. We said goodnight to Ron and went out into the front lobby. I opened the briefcase and checked the oil vials, but there was nothing wrong. They were intact and unbroken, and the smell was gone.

Then it came to me that the smell was coming from the presence of the Lord inside the prison.

WOW!

The Kirby Man

We were blessed with a free demonstration and carpet cleaning using the Kirby Vacuum machine.

The Kirby man and his apprentice came and explained his machine. He claimed that it would clean better than any other machine in the world. He showed us where our carpet pile was dirty, crushed down and trapping in dirt that had been responsible for destroying its life. Dirt had crept in particle by particle until it was filled. Loaded with dirt the pile had been crushed and bent over. This actually trapped dirt and prevented it from being cleaned out. Our conventional methods of cleaning only touched the surface. It did nothing to rid the pile of the trapped-in dirt nor did it bring new life to the crushed pile. It remained crushed and only looked clean on the surface.

With a power-packed motor and excellent design, the machine vacuumed with more capacity than any other. Its power reached down inside the pile and pulled up 95% of the embedded dirt that all the other vacuums had left behind. It also dispensed a dry foam that soaked the pile with cleansing power. Then the machine brushed the carpet and the cleaner pile began to stand up after years of being crushed and bent over by dirt. The machine can now vacuum out more dirt which was trapped in the bent-over pile because the carpet pile is in an upright position—whereupon new life is brought to the carpet as the pile is able to stand on its own again in a renewed or reborn fashion.

A carpet that was at the end of its life in the eyes of the world and ready to be torn out and scrapped is reborn and given a new life by the Kirby man and his wonderful machine.

As I sat on our stairs watching the Kirby man, God began to speak to me and show me that this is what He does in the lives of people. People that are crushed and burdened with sin trapped in their lives hear the Gospel, the Good News of Jesus Christ, and invite God to come into their lives. He reaches down with the power of the Cross and removes their sins as far as the end of the east is from the end of the west. They are washed clean by the blood of Jesus and the Water of the Word. As they are reborn and stand up in righteousness they open up to even deeper purification and cleansing of their hearts and souls.

As with the reborn carpet, the Kirby machine continues to maintain carpet pile, so with reborn Christians God continues in our lives to keep us healthy and clean.

The Kirby man came to our door because someone that cares about us decided to bless us with a free demonstration. The Kirby man and God both come empowered with good news that is confirmed with signs and wonders resulting in new life for the downtrodden.

Our thanks to Mark and Susie Wheeler for the blessing of the Kirby Man.

Our thanks to God for confirming His Gospel in our lives.

"Being confident of this, that He who began a good work in you will carry it on to completion until the day of Christ Jesus."

Phil 1:6

End of a Chapter: The Death of Agnes

Cancer came in the spring of 1999 and consumed much of our lives for five and a half years. During that time Agnes remained a functional Prison Minister. After operations midweek, she would lead the Church Service Sunday night, directing music worship, with baggy clothes covering drainage tubes and bandages. Towards the end she was confined to a wheelchair. Only during the last two weeks of her life was she bedridden and unable to go into the prison.

In early 2004 she went through her last operation, and then in June and July she went through her last chemo and radiation treatments. She was given prednisone to counteract the physically draining effect of the treatments, and by August she was through with treatment and strengthened by the prednisone.

Pastor Bob Emery, a close friend, informed me that he was arranging a one week free vacation for Agnes and me on Prince Edward Island. We only had to choose the week. It was a gift from the Christian Community that knew and supported us. We both knew August was the time to go on vacation while Agnes was strong enough to enjoy it.

All expenses were paid, which included air travel from Montreal, a rental car at Prince Edward Island, a cabin on the bay, and $3,200 cash in my pocket.

What a great time we had enjoying the cabin on the bay and traveling around the Island. We watched locals harvesting Irish Moss, a type of seaweed that washes up on the shore. Teams of horses dragged a large rake on the beaches to gather it. Extracts from the Irish Moss are used in foods like ice cream, and local restaurants serve Irish Moss Pie that looks and tastes like Key Lime Pie.

Prince Edward Island is famous for growing Yukon Gold Potatoes and for the stories of Anne of Green Gables. They also manufacture and sell top of the line stainless steel cookware. We bought the same set that Airforce One had.

By the end of the week I had failed to spend the $3200—we could only eat so many lobsters, Irish Moss pies, and clams were free for the digging on the beaches. We had a great and memorable time there.

After coming home from our Prince Edward Island vacation, Agnes started to deteriorate fast. Eventually, she was confined to a wheelchair. One of our clients brought us a battery-powered wheel chair so Agnes could get around and we could still go for walks on the bike trail.

Agnes continued to go into the prison with me in a wheel chair and direct music worship with her worship team. She also traveled to Barre with me to attend a Board of Directors Meeting at Pastor Herb Hatch's home, though toward the end of the meeting she had to retire to the bedroom for a nap.

I remember being upset as I watched her weaken. One day I went for a walk on the walking path. As I was trying to pray, I yelled out to God, "What's going on?" He answered me immediately: "I am preparing you for the death of your wife." At that moment I became silent and shut down. I believed Him and accepted that Agnes would soon die. Part of me was dying also. I can't describe it other than inside I was shutting down.

Her last time inside the prison was November 7, 2004. After that she was bedridden. She had one last visit with a doctor who gave her one last CT Scan. Afterwards, the doc called and said the cancer had spread to her liver, which meant her life would end soon.

The family was notified and everyone from out of state came to see her. Nathan, Edita and Danny had already moved in with us and were helping to run the household. Visiting nurses came and assisted with Agnes' care—one of whom told me I could apply extra morphine patches to her to better mitigate the pain and nobody would know.

When my father was dying from cancer in Porter Hospital in Middlebury, the doctor said, "Do you want me to help your father along?" He explained that he could give him an extra shot that would end the pain and speed up the process of dying. I thought about it, and prayed, deciding that nothing should be done to end or prolong his life intentionally. I wanted to treat him for pain, but leave the rest up to God. I remember my father's body shutting down as he was dying. His extremities grew cold as his heartbeat faded and his breathing slowed down. Then it all stopped.

Agnes was receiving morphine for pain in various forms and at different times. The hardest instance for me was when the morphine dulled her mind and she couldn't communicate well. She was confused, so I put her in the wheelchair and took her to the back enclosed porch, where we sat for a while. She had her journal and a pen, but was not able to write. I knew this meant she was very confused and suffering in her mind, so I stopped using that form of morphine and went back to a previous form that allowed her mind to be clear and able to communicate.

Nathan and Edita had decided they wanted their wedding to be sooner than planned, while Agnes was still able to do the ceremony. Originally the wedding was to be at the First Baptist Church on Congress Street in St. Albans. I let Nathan know that Agnes wouldn't be with us much longer and that the wedding should be very soon. So on Thanksgiving Day, November 25, 2004, I printed out a simple one page wedding ceremony. Edita descended the staircase—a beautiful bride in a beautiful wedding dress—and they entered the bedroom, now dubbed the "Agnes Fiske Chapel."

The ceremony began, and Agnes began to read, stumbling over a few words. She looked at me and said, "Should I start over?" I said, "No, honey. Look at them. It's working." She looked at their smiling faces and continued. We all cheered as she presented Mr. and Mrs. Nathan Fiske to our family and friends.

Pastor Agnes, aka Mom, gave the couple her best pastoral advice: "Take lots of showers together!" History may or may not reveal whether they took that advice or not. She also said, "Have children." That advice definitely worked. In 2007 they had twin boys: Noah and Nicholas.

The next day Pastor Duane Hodgeman came to see Agnes for the last time. He wept profusely. She told him she was ready to go, saying, "All accounts are settled!" By which she meant family accounts. She could leave in peace because there were no outstanding issues.

Agnes had known that she was "The Bride of Christ" from the first time she read it in the Bible. That she "knew that she knew" was her way of saying she had 100% belief. Since then, she had wanted to be buried in a wedding dress for her groom Jesus. She had only been "on loan" to me, from Him, for 39 years, from 1965 (our first *blind* date) until Nov 30, 2004.

On Monday morning we knew she was not going to last another day, so Edita and I went to Needleman's Bridal Store on Main Street in St. Albans and bought a slender white wedding dress. We came back to the house and hung it up on the door of the bedroom. Agnes regained consciousness long enough to see it and nod her head in approval. Then she closed her eyes for the last time. She was prepared to meet her Groom.

As her breathing became labored, I put a chair beside her bed and held her hand. When the day turned into evening, my son Nathan took care of my needs and checked on me regularly. I asked God to take me with her. I believe God's answer to that prayer was "No" and He took me out of the picture in a strange way.

At 11:58 p.m. Nathan opened the door and asked if I needed anything. I said, "No, thank you" and closed my eyes. I opened my eyes again and it was 12:02 a.m. Four minutes had elapsed, and during that time Agnes had passed into the arms of her Groom Jesus. Her eyelids were open, so I kissed her and closed them. Then I went into the living room and sat down in a chair and let everyone know.

> And at midnight a cry was heard: 'Behold, the bridegroom is coming; go out to meet him!' Then all those virgins arose and trimmed their lamps. And the foolish said to the wise, 'Give us some of your oil, for our lamps are going out.' But the wise answered, saying, 'No, lest there should not be enough for us and you; but go rather to those who sell, and buy for yourselves.' And while they went to buy, the bridegroom came, and those who were ready went in with him to the wedding; and the door was shut (*Matthew 25:6-10*).

Jesus honored her faith and came exactly as Agnes expected, on time! At the midnight hour! On her dresser was an oil lamp with the wick trimmed and filled with oil. She was ready to leave with Jesus.

Memories of Agnes

The following is an account by Eileen (Burnor) Drew, entitled "Memories of Agnes' Last Weekend with Us before She Went Home to The Lord."

As I recall, a few of us close friends gathered at Pete and Agnes' home in St. Albans and surrounded Agnes in her bed. Louie St. Cyr sang one of Agnes' favorite songs, "The Anchor Holds." She was more alert at some times than others, but I know she was aware of our presence surrounding her.

She always maintained a sweet presence through all she suffered, even to her very last moments before leaving us. She clearly had oil in her lamp and the wick was ready. She had left clear instructions for which dress she was to have on for her home going. It was a bridal gown of her choosing.

Not long before that, as her last official pastoral act, Pastor Agnes had the opportunity to officiate her youngest son's wedding. I remember she gave the couple clear instructions to bring forth children. They were obedient to her request and twin sons were born to them within the next few years.

A few hours after we left, Agnes went to be with her Savior face-to-face and became part of the great cloud of witnesses. Her life positively impacted the lives of countless people, both before and during her prison ministry, and she left a blessed legacy for her family.

She was a steadfast and faithful servant of the Lord, and I don't doubt He welcomed her home with, "Well done good and faithful servant."

We look forward to that wonderful day when we will see her again.

"Precious in the sight of the Lord is the death of saints."

Psalm 116:15

❖

The following account of Agnes is by Diane St. Cyr.

I met Agnes through a mutual friend and loved her from that moment on. Agnes was involved in a prison Ministry with her husband Pete. She was the "heart" of the ministry and a mother figure to many who was both respected and adored. Because she had raised a family of boys, Agnes was a natural with the young men,

My husband Louie and I were in a small home group with Pete and Agnes, so we were family. Upon hearing about her diagnosis of cancer, we were heartbroken. We prayed for her, over her and with her, beseeching God's mercy. Still, the illness progressed. On the last day of Agnes' life on earth, we received a phone call from Pete saying she had asked for Louie to sing "The Anchor Holds" for her. Louie did not hesitate. We jumped in the car and drove to St. Albans. Louie sat by her bed, held her hand, and sang to her as her beloved family wept silently.

It was a Holy moment we will never forget.

No matter what life brought Agnes, she met every challenge, heartache and disappointment with faith and courage. Like a ship on a raging sea, the cancer had taken its toll. But the Anchor steadied and held her.

She knew that Jesus, the rock of her salvation and the bridegroom who adored her, was waiting at the end of her journey.

❖

The following account of Agnes is by our son Adam.

Mom,

To the one who gave me life and taught me hope, love, and faith. I thank you most of all for teaching me how to love without worry or regret. You taught me how to hope for things that might not come to pass and for things that will.

You taught me to have faith in things that cannot be seen, heard, touched or spoken to. Because of you I am who I am, forgiving, loving, hopeful and above all faithful to myself and my loved ones. For that I thank you.

Adam P. Fiske
11/24/04

The Funeral

I said my last goodbye to Agnes at her funeral. My friend Roger Patno's wife Joyce had passed away from cancer in August, and Roger was able to preach at Joyce's funeral. I couldn't do that. I was so shut down I could barely talk. Pastor Duane Hodgeman officiated.

Our two inmate Pastors, Fred Little and Ramon Valentine, were allowed to attend the funeral, which they did in orange jumpsuits and shackles. Both men came to the podium and spoke to the assembly on my behalf, and as close confidants and friends-in-Christ of Agnes. I was proud of them and thanked God they were able to attend. They were the highlight of that day for me.

Many people from our Christian community attended alongside members of the Department of Corrections—for Agnes was highly respected and loved by many.

Her casket was arranged so that she was facing east, where the sun rises above Mount Mansfield.

> "For as the lightning comes from the east and flashes to the west,
> so also will the coming of the Son of Man be."
>
> *Matt 24:7*

On the west wall of the church, where the sun set in the evening, there was a banner that God had used to speak to her concerning attending United Christian Assembly. He had said "This is where I want you." The banner proclaimed, "Create in Me a Clean Heart, oh God." *Psalm 51:10*

At the graveside my friend, Reverend Roger Patno, did the internment service. Afterwards he came to me as I watched the casket being lowered into the ground, and said, "Peter! You know she is no longer here. You know where she is now." Somehow those words released me from the grave. Having graduated from this life and entered into Heaven for eternity, she was now with her bridegroom, Jesus.

I knew Agnes was received with a grand reception there, in her new home.

July 2, 1978 Agnes turned away from the world and received Jesus as her Lord and Savior. "I tell you, there is rejoicing in the presence of the angels of God over one sinner who repents." *Luke 15:10.* How much more rejoicing was there as she arrived with her Bridegroom Jesus?

A Christian friend had a vision of Agnes being greeted by Joyce Patno, who said, "Come in Agnes. It's beautiful here."

A New Chapter Begins: The Hand

After Agnes passed I sold the house in St Albans the following July (2005). Nathan and I bought a nice house together in Swanton. It was a 3 bedroom ranch with an attached 3 room apartment where I lived. There was a hallway leading to a door into the main house. I would have supper with Nathan, Edita, Danny and Hasnija (Edita's mother visiting from Bosnia). However, I was not doing well as a single man.

Nate's two dogs would come visit me in my apartment and share snacks with me as I sat in my recliner chair. I was gaining weight and eventually reached 246 pounds. Even though I was still an active Prison Pastor and ministering to released inmates also, I was feeling dead inside. After the Prince Edward Island vacation with Agnes when God told me, "I am preparing you for the death of your wife," I had shut down inside. I had accepted Agnes' death as God's plan and continuation of my life alone.

One evening after supper we were all in the living room watching a movie on the TV. The lights were off, Nathan and Edita were sitting on the couch to the right of me, Danny and his grandmother Hasnija were sitting on the love seat to my left. I was in the middle reclining on a Chaise Lounge chair.

Suddenly I saw a hand appear out of the darkness, just to the left of my face. It moved downward and stroked my bare right arm. It delivered a soft, gentle feminine touch, and then it retreated back up into the darkness.

I don't remember being excited and telling everybody what had just happened. I do remember feeling that God was telling me that my time of mourning was over and it was not good for me to be alone. It was time to go on with my life.

Then the Lord God said, "It is not good for the man to be alone. I will make a helper who is just right for him" (*Genesis 2:18*).

Hello Joanne Falise

by Joanne "Jo" Fiske

Today, March 19th, 2024 is my birthday. However, today I am remembering March 18th, 2006. It was Marian Fay's funeral at Essex Alliance. Pastor Pete Fiske sat in the row in front of me as I listened to Pastor Fred Little speak and was blown away by the Holy Spirit (God's presence) in him. Fred was an inmate at Northwest State Correctional Facility where he had been ordained as senior pastor of the Church at Northwest. He was dressed in prison clothing and shackled as he spoke about Marian, who at the age of 92 had still been a volunteer at the prison, blind and in a wheelchair. She would meet with Fred and others every Wednesday for Bible study and prayer. She had told Fred that they would be "Forever Friends," extending into eternity. He said her faithful visits each week were the "ministry of presence," a term I came to appreciate.

But most of all I heard what God said to me about Pete: "This is a man you can trust." I was very drawn to those comforting words. Having been in an abusive marriage and turbulent relationships, I'd told Jesus He was my husband, that I did not need an earthly one because of the past.

I was a realtor at the time, and Pete and I spoke after the service about real estate, then we both got up and mingled. I remember looking for Pete a while later and seeing him from a distance go out the door. I ran after him, but he was gone, and I felt a deep sense of disappointment. However, we connected by email the next day, on my birthday, March 19th, 2006, and so it began ... our love story!

As our emails became more personal, we decided to meet in person to determine if God had a plan for our relationship. I made it clear that I was vulnerable and not interested in dating for fun, but rather seeing each other to learn what God might have in store for us.

Eventually Pastor Pete stopped by my condo for coffee mid-morning on his way to run an errand in the area. We chatted, but I was concerned about what neighbors might think of me, a single woman, having a man in my house for too long. Before he left, he asked, "Would you like to go to church with me this Sunday? It's an evening service." Little did I know he meant his church inside prison.

When the day came, driving to the prison in St. Albans felt weird and nerve-racking. Even more so when we went inside, going through a metal detector and leaving our belongings in a locker. We followed a big intimidating-looking officer through a locked door down a dimly fluorescent lit hallway to another locked door. After going through the next door, Pastor Pete asked a man in a glassed-in area to please call out the church service. Navigating from a confusing hallway crossroads area with about seven doors, we went through one of the doors into a room that was about 30' x 50'. Folding chairs were set up facing the back, and to the left was a row of mid-height windows that stretched to the ceiling. The sight of razor wires atop a metal fence through the windows reminded me of the severity of the institution I was presently standing in, luckily as a visitor.

The inmates slowly filed into the room in groups of two and three, about 30 men, until they filled the room. Pastor Fred Little was there; his warm smile calmed my jitters, and Pastor Pete was a reassuring presence by my side. However, I soon realized that in church these men were not felons, robbers and worse, but people, like me, there to worship God and seek to become more like Jesus. There was a live band, Andy Wood played guitar and sang. Then Pastor Pete asked me to introduce myself, and though I was shaking inside, I felt more at home there than I had in a long time.

I belonged.

Our first date was in prison, and I was with the man God wanted me to be with. One who I could trust and would eventually marry. I never stopped going to Pastor Pete's church at prison on Sundays and eventually led Bible studies, shared in pastoral counseling alongside Pete, got involved in aftercare and so much more. I even started a satellite college from an accredited institution and facilitated 16 courses. I can honestly say that those years were the best in my life. It is a humbling opportunity and an awesome privilege to share in the lives of so many and do what this one sheep can do to help lead others to the Shephard.

Thank you, Lord!

Thank you, Peter Fiske, my knight in shining armor for sharing your life with me.

The River of Life to Jesus
Vs.
The Downward Landslide into The Abyss

I had a vision that I can still see to this day; a vision of the entire earth slipping down a mountain in a landslide of moral and spiritual wickedness, down to an abyss that will eventually swallow it up. No one realizes it because everyone in the landslide sees each other, and since they are all going in the same direction they have no other reference point. On the top of the mountain is Jesus and we believers are walking up to Him as the earth slides downward past us.

I shared the vision with Jo, and God inspired her with this interpretation:

"But those who know Jesus are walking in a shallow river-way, a highway of Holiness going up a long steep hill in the opposite direction, joyfully walking, skipping, running upward towards Jesus.

It's not always easy because there are slippery rocks and potholes, but we struggle along. We are splashing each other with the water which is like washing the dirt and dust of our sins off with the Water of the Word of God, and we are going as fast as we can because the time is short.

As we go we are reaching over into the crowds of those on the downhill avalanche and grabbing people as fast as we can and splashing them and helping them as they stumble but begin to march and at
times run with us up this highway of holiness made up of the river of life coming from the throne room of God. And as the people go down the hill oblivious to almost everything else, some are trying to pull us over with them, some are shooting arrows or spears to try to kill us, but there are angels

blocking them. We get weak sometimes so then we drink the water and are refreshed.

Those who don't splash or drink enough are getting tired, weary and some fall off or decide it's too hard and allow the ones on the downhill slide to pull them into the fray with them and they are lost. Some get snatched back up by others downstream, and when they drink and splash their strength and joy is renewed. I could go on, but all this to say, and I know it from experience, that when we don't read the word, sing songs, hang with other Christians, and go to church to be with others enough we grow weary from the fight of resisting the worldly temptations, which seem pleasurable at first but only lead to sorrow."

The Vacuum Cleaner

Jo lost a part to her cell phone yesterday so I took a flashlight and, using an advanced never-before-revealed-to-the-world oblique lighting technique, searched the floors and under the furniture. Overcome with horror at the dust, dog and cat hair, and pine needle buildup on the floor, I searched fervently for the lost item. All I found was the unsavory realization that the forest comes in with our animals and is spread throughout the home glued to dog and cat hair!

What a revelation for a husband!

What a mess!

This morning I couldn't get the gruesome images of dirt and unspeakable detritus beneath the furniture out of my mind ... I knew God was prompting me to vacuum, so I pulled out the old banged-up vacuum cleaner. Dented, scuffed, miscolored—every part worn, broken, not working or missing. Yes, we had a maintenance contract and could get it repaired at no cost. But after years of slogging up and downstairs, jamming against walls, and cramming into corners, it had grown old and weather-worn.

How much nicer to have a shiny new machine!

Then, suddenly, God said, "Peter, you are aging also. Your parts are worn, broken, not working correctly or missing too. But the vacuum cleaner is still doing what it was designed to do. It is still sucking up dirt and making noises that scare the dog. Likewise, you are still able to do what I designed you to do. You can think and speak and interact with others. I have purpose for you for another ten years. You will speak for Me and do what I have anointed you to do."

"But Lord, I have labored for you for a quarter century. I need time with our children."

"I will give you time with your children, and I will bless them because of you and your labor for Me. Stay in your anointing, walking the anointed path I have given you."

God restored me to my family in my Jubilee year—my 50th birthday party at a family reunion. By then I had labored 28 years at IBM and 22 years in Prison Ministry. That's 50 years. Half a century. My Jubilee of laboring! IBM prepared me to work with the Vermont Department of Corrections ... and survive.

But the next ten years with Jo would be the most productive years for us, our family members and for God's Kingdom.

Yes Lord, Yes Lord, Yes Lord!

Spring is Here and So is The Upper Room

by Joanne "Jo" Fiske

With a new husband who is a prison minister comes a new way of life for the former Joanne "Jo" Falise. Before December 30, 2006 she was single with no family living in VT, and— although her real estate business and duties as a deaconess in her church and president of her condo association kept her extremely busy—her home was empty and lonely.

I had recently experienced the death of my Mom, my best friend who went home to be with the Lord after a long battle with cancer, and then both of my golden retrievers, my close companions for fifteen years, passed. It was tough coming home to an empty house. But I poured myself into real estate and clung to *Phil 4:11* "I have learned in whatever situation I am to be content…"

Then I met Pastor Pete at Marian Fay's funeral, thank you Marian. While we were dating, God gave Pastor Pete the scripture from the *Song of Solomon 2:10-13*. A portion of that says: "… for behold, the winter is past; the rain is over and gone. The flowers appear on the earth, the time of singing has come…" And I can truly say after four months of marriage, the Lord answered the deepest cry of my heart and filled my life to overflowing with the blessing of serving Him by my husband's side in the Church At Prison. I am only beginning to learn the depth and intense needs of this prison ministry that I have grown to love.

God has also blessed me with a large wonderful new family here in Vermont, with more in other states, to add to my own. I even have two new four legged furry friends, Alex and Mitty, to populate my home. And the extra bedroom upstairs in our condo is no longer just a place to store things, it has now become an "Upper Room" for visitors, including new grandchildren, Christian friends from Nigeria, a Bishop from Pakistan, ministry staff, and those released from prison intent on walking a good path. What a joy for this upper room to now be a safe sanctuary and place of rest for so many.

This Easter our home was filled with family, the fragrant aromas of baked ham, candied sweet potatoes, turnips, asparagus, mashed potatoes, corn bread, and the coos of three week-old twin grandsons, Nicholas and Noah, the newest of 13 grandchildren I can now call my own. As I write this I am choked with tears of joy for how the Lord has answered my simple prayer in secret with Him ... that it be His will to bring me a husband in full-time ministry to Him.

God knew what He was doing as he prepared me for this specific ministry through many varied and horrendously difficult life experiences, but through which he was giving me skills to be a more effective mate to Pastor Pete in this ministry. The Church At Northwest and all the men there as well as the volunteers have become my family as well, and I know this is where I belong.

I know that God has called me into this place with my husband and best friend Pastor Pete. I am deeply humbled and grateful that I have been given the privilege to be of service in some small way to the Church At Prison.

Isaiah 40 Vision

While driving to Barre pick up a client, I prayed, "Lord let me see things the way you see them."

Immediately, the road in front of me rose and heaved with large rippling waves and the edges of the pavement broke up in pieces. In the breakdown lane on the side of the highway a car had pulled over with its flashers on. As I continued to drive the terrain beneath the car remained smooth.

Then the words roared in my head: "The earth is quaking beneath our feet. God is calling us to get our eyes on Jesus. He is on the way!" It was my sermon the Lord gave me.

On the way back from Barre the same vision repeated.

The next day as Jo and I drove south on I-89 to Springfield Prison, the rippling road loomed in front of me once again, and another car appeared in the breakdown lane with its flashers on. I wondered what God was saying and shared my vision with several other people.

Jo asked if I had prayed and asked God directly.

I had not.

So we prayed and I was reminded of the scripture wherein John the Baptist was talking about preparing the way for the Lord. Jo looked up *Mathew 3:1-3* "He is a voice shouting in the wilderness, 'Prepare the way for the LORD's coming! Clear the road for him!' The voice of one crying in the wilderness, 'Prepare ye the way of the Lord, make his paths straight.'"

Then Jo looked up *Isaiah 40:3-4*

The voice of one crying in the wilderness: "Prepare the way of the Lord; Make straight in the desert a highway for our God. Every valley shall be exalted And every mountain and hill brought low; The crooked places shall be made straight And the rough places smooth…"

Then the Lord spoke to Jo and she told me: "The Lord is saying keep going, don't stop or grow weary. I am with you now. I will never leave you nor forsake you. Lo, I am with you even to the end of the age! Press in and I will be your God, your strength. 'I will cause you to rise up as on wings of eagles, you shall walk and not grow weary, run and not grow faint.' I will make a way through the ripples and bumps and mountains. Can I not do it? Only believe!

"Shout My name. Proclaim My word and truth by the power of the Holy Spirit.

"My word is the power to save. Tell everyone.

"Don't stop or get discouraged."

IV.

LESSONS FROM THE FOREST

God Speaks

"Henceforth you will hear a word behind you, saying, 'This is the way, walk in it.'"

Isaiah 30:21

When Joanne bought her condo in Jericho one of the reasons for that location was the forest with hiking trails connecting to the back yard. Once we started seeing each other Joanne took me out on the trails to "break me in." We also started hiking on the Bamforth Ridge at the North End of Camels Hump. The first time up was a two mile hike on a very hard trail. At the end of the day I weighed myself and discovered I had lost 7 pounds.

After we married I moved into the condo, which was a better choice than my three room in-law-apartment in Swanton; although living with my son Nathan and his family had been critical for my wellbeing after the death of Agnes. As I became accustomed to my new home I began to go for late night and early morning walks using a headlamp. During one of my walks one night I needed direction from God and wanted Him to speak to me. I was very determined and stood still, leaning on my walking staff, and said, "Lord I need to hear you speak to me. I am not moving until you speak." A few minutes later God spoke to me mind and said, "Start walking and turn left at the next intersection." There were many crisscrossing paths throughout the forest, but from that moment on He would tell me where to turn each time I asked.

A couple years later I walked out to the trail late at night and there were two deer watching me from the forest. I asked God which way to go and He said go left, then right, and then right again. The deer began walking parallel to me as I went down the trail. I turned right and they were still there among the trees as I walked. I turned right again as God had told me. I was watching Alex, our German Shepard, as she had her nose to the ground taking in all the smells on the trail, but unaware of the deer. I looked up to see if the deer were still nearby and was startled to see I was surrounded by 11 pairs of eyes glowing in the light of my headlight. My whole body was tingling as I looked at all the deer looking at me. They were 20 to 40 feet from me on both sides of the trail. Alex kept her nose to the ground, sniffing, and never knew the deer were there. We kept walking so as not to disturb them.

On July 2, 1978 I saw a doe and fawn, and God said, "Peter this is a sign of your new life." Was this a hint from God as to what was to come nearly 30 years later?

What a blessing!

And so my lessons in the forest began.

Life is Like a Forest

"Come to me, all of you who are weary and carry heavy burdens, and I will give you rest. Take my yoke upon you. Let me teach you, because I am humble and gentle at heart, and you will find rest for your souls. For my yoke is easy to bear, and the burden I give you is light."

Mathew 11:28-30

Life is like walking blind into a forest. Taking one step at a time into the dark, when you progress diligently and your foot hits a root, you rebalance yourself and step carefully over it. When you proceed too fast and reckless, you trip.

Sometimes, try as you might, you lose the path.

Bump!

You run into a tree trunk and hit your nose. A little blood! You wipe it off and step to the right, then continue moving forward again. You learn to sense the trees by the rise of the ground under your feet, the earth arching over their roots. Ever so slowly you are learning to walk into the dark forest.

Thump!

You trip over a rock and down you go.

Ouch!

As you bang your knee on the sharp rock. Rubbing the bruise, you get up and learn to step more carefully, navigating forward by putting your weight on your foot after it is securely in place.

Suddenly your hear a hoot! hoot! followed by a whoosh! as an owl dives down from its unseen perch above and glides right over your naked head. Startled you duck, but the owl has deftly maneuvered around you to its target, and you turn to see the baby rabbit carried upwards into the forest canopy.

Continuing on your way, your foot swiftly slides uncontrollably upon the ground and out from under your body as you slip on a spot of ice that was hidden beneath a pile of pine needles that have insulated the ground and kept it from thawing.

Oof!

Landing sideways on your hip you pause to lay still for a moment, hoping to determine that you have not broken a bone. Once this first stage of recovery has been completed, you scan your body more intently to assess whether you've sustained an injury or are just mildly bruised and sore.

Then you rise up slowly, now exceedingly vigilant in avoiding the ice, and continue with a slight limp in your gait compensating for a mild bruise. You realize you've been affected by the fall, but are now wiser to circumvent the myriad forms of treachery that dwell throughout the forest.

For somewhere out there in the darkness you know there is a cliff that others have stumbled over, falling unawares to an early death. They were rushing ahead, living life in fast forward, seeking immediate gratification of their desirous impulses. Not willing to be patient and lacking wisdom, they sped down the pathway that leads to self-destruction. And, having entirely lost the pathway to life, there are some falls from which there is no recovery. No getting up again.

The pitfalls and perils, snags and snares are all waiting for you in the forest. The impossible situations and bewildering people. The uncanny circumstances and dastardly deceptions. You can't avoid running into them, but you can practice wisdom. You can move ahead on the gradual path, remembering God at each step on the way. You can't avoid mishaps and mistakes, but you can learn from them, do your best to survive, and gain a bit more clarity and wisdom with each lesson learned.

We will always encounter situations beyond our control and be challenged to make the right choice. With work, marriage, friends, and fortune, life is a constant testing ground in which we must exercise our intelligence and seek the righteous path. But sometimes making the right decision is not as easy or important as making our decisions right after we see the errors and consequences of our ways.

Life is like a forest.

There will be bumps, bruises, and predators ... all forcing us to make choices that come with consequences. Life can become overly burdensome and difficult when we forget God. But when we remember Him and the grace He extends to us through the turmoils and tribulations of each day, our path becomes a little brighter and our load lighter.

The Pathway (Coyotes I)

After a midnight walk I am on the deck, listening to a pack of coyotes howling back and forth in the forest as they hunt game. It is good that we got back home earlier and our cat Shiloh is in the house as he would make a tasty morsel for the pack.

I look into the darkness of the forest from my well-lit deck and see nothing, but I can hear them. Then the pack grows silent as they glide like grey shadows through the nighttime forest. Maybe they are watching us, hoping to grab Shiloh. My neighbor Fran, later that day, told me that she and her boyfriend also heard them in the trees beyond Jo's flower garden. 50 feet from our deck, looking and watching for Shiloh? Were you scared? I asked. "Nope!" she replied. "I'm packing!" Fran was a Homeland Security Officer.

Earlier that evening the Lord had said, "Turn your headlight off" as I was on the lawn preparing to enter the forest. So I walked in the forest tonight without my headlight. The Lord had taken away my fear of the dark many years ago as He prepared me for a life in ministry, a life lived by faith and not by sight. "This is my command—be strong and courageous! Do not be afraid or discouraged. For the Lord your God is with you wherever you go" (*Joshua 1:9*).

Leaving the home sanctuary I entered the dark forest through the gateway. As I got farther from the light of the house, I could see less, but Alex apparently had no problem seeing and sniffing her way down the narrow path that leads from our house to the main trail. "Narrow is the trail that leads to life and few are they that find it" (*Matthew 7:14*) I am on that narrow trail and Alex is at the other end of the leash gently leading me—as Shiloh trots just behind us, knowing that predators lurk in the night.

Normally on our walks Alex goes on and off the path, smelling and sniffing the scents on bushes, trees, stumps and clumps of weeds. Tonight she is on the leash, purposely staying on the path, gently pulling me forward in tune with God's purpose.

She knows I can't see in the dark, and gently pulls as I follow as she turns right between two trees where the path is narrow and constricting. I can feel the depth of the trail and the edges where they rise. A root here and bump there, and I adjust my steps. My confidence in Alex as my guide is limited, and I know a right turn is coming. If we miss it I will stumble over a log and fall in a brush pile. Maybe a limb will poke me in the eye. I sense that log is near, so I decide it's time to turn on the light before Alex leads me into trouble.

Alas, where I am is not where I expected to be, but much farther out than I thought. Alex has led me between trees, between two jagged stumps with only 10 inches of clearance between them, around sharp corners and out of the narrow path onto the main trail. She navigated a major corner where the path turned left and another where it turned right, leading us through a narrow opening cut in a fallen log without me knowing it.

With a degree in mechanical engineering design and drafting I am very aware of straight lines, level surfaces and angles. During our walk I know we went in a straight line on level ground. How was it that I turned corners and walked over bumps and dips in the path without knowing it?

Then I remembered God speaking through Jo from *Isaiah 40:3-4:*

> The voice of one crying in the wilderness: "Prepare the way of the Lord; Make straight in the desert a highway for our God. Every valley shall be exalted And every mountain and hill brought low; The crooked places shall be made straight And the rough places smooth…"

God told us to continue our work for Him and He would clear the way and guide us. This evening God gave me a physical demonstration of what He was doing for us.

Wow!

Continuing on, Alex and I walked by the old Pine giants, where tree frogs called out to each other in the night. I wondered how such a small frog could make such a loud sound. Listening to them chirp, I reviewed the lessons learned on the walk.

Have confidence in the guidance God provides. Don't push too fast. It is not speed that produces fruit, it is focus, paying attention, observing details, listening to the tree frogs, and following the guide God gave me.

The Short Leash

"The people who walk in darkness will see a great light. For those who live in a land of deep darkness, a light will shine."

Isaiah 9:2

It is 4:30 a.m. and the Lord has called me again to rise and come out into the forest. It is dark as Alex and I leave the light of the house and walk into darkness. As the light from the house recedes behind us, darkness brings danger and I keep Alex on a short leash.

Soon the Son is rising in the east with its gift of light, and in the dusky glow of the approaching dawn, the pathway is visible.

I see there was a storm in the night that brought tree limbs down and scattered forest trash throughout the pathway. Inevitably, some limbs wrenched from the trees did not reach the forest floor and became stuck in the canopy. My father, Bob Fiske, the Tree Man of Addison County, called them "dead men" because of their propensity to fall unannounced upon unsuspecting walkers-by. Most woodsmen call them "widow-makers" for much the same reason.

Alex's short leash ensures she won't get tangled in the chaotic mess. She submits to the limitation upon her freedom because, over all, she enjoys the journey through the woods. She doesn't understand that it is for her protection. She only knows that I am in charge and that the short lease is one of the conditions she must accept to accompany me on the walk.

As we tread through areas of intense destruction and disarray in the forest I keep the leash short and tight. When we come to areas that are open and clear I loosen the leash to full length and she trots on ahead, enjoying the freedom to sniff out and explore areas of interest.

In much the same way that I look out for Alex and regulate her freedom to guide her and keep her safe, so the Lord provides me with the guidance and direction I need, keeping me on a leash that provides optimal stewardship of my wanderings. Sometimes the leash seems too short and I become frustrated, wanting greater freedom and exploration. But God knows what's best for me. He knows when there are dangerous forces working against His purpose.

The more I trust Him, the more secure I am in His hands (*John 10:29b*).

The Little Dog

In early winter our German Shepard, Alex, attacked and killed a large possum who had wandered into our back yard. During January Thaw of the same year, we discovered where she had buried her treasure in the melted snow bank. I collected the dead possum, which was gruesome with blood and attack wounds on its neck, put it in a plastic bag and disposed of it.

Not long after that Jo and I were walking in the forest behind our home and encountered a neighbor who was walking her little white dog. Unexpectedly, Alex began to growl then attacked the little dog viciously as if she was trying to kill it. After breaking them apart, the trembling neighbor took her little dog in her arms and went to the vet where the dog was treated. $120 later, with antibiotics and stitches, the dog recovered. After this, we promised not to let Alex off-leash again while walking in the forest, and I began to take her out after dark when I knew other dogs would not be around.

Three months later I was in New Hampshire presenting a Safe Sanctuary Seminar for a group of churches wanting to work with released sexual offenders. Jo took Alex out for a walk on the leash, and all was going well until they came to our favorite spot—a place where the path descends into a steep gulley and rises up the other side. The game we played here was as much fun for us as it was for Alex: we would make Alex stay at the crest of the gulley while we lumbered down and back up the slope to the far crest. From there we would scream out for her to come and cheer her on enthusiastically as she ran pell-mell to catch up with us.

Unable to contain her zeal for fun, on the walk Jo let Alex off-leash at the gulley to play our game. However, as Alex was running wildly to her, out of nowhere the little white dog appeared and she zoned it and attacked! She was so fervent in her endeavors to destroy the poor creature that Jo scooped up the little dog as the other person drove Alex away. Regrettably, the little dog was once again injured.

Needless to say, all the promises and apologies in the world did not help to remediate the situation.

When I returned home from my seminar I took Alex out after dark on her leash, which she had bitten in two and escaped a couple years previously—the two ends now tied together. A two-time offender and escapist. High-risk and now high-profile in the neighborhood. We had already drawn ire and uprisings in our community due to the "dangerous" clients we brought to our house. Now we were rebuked for our German Shepard!

Reflecting upon the situation, I realized this little white dog was the only dog Alex had ever attacked. But why? Then it dawned on me: the little dog looked a lot like that possum Alex had killed as part and parcel of protecting her homestead. The battle with the possum had been emblazoned in Alex's memory such that, via association, upon encountering the little white dog she saw a threatening possum invading her territory—so she went into bloodthirsty Braveheart mode and attacked! And now she had offended twice! And escaped as a fugitive once. All these factors made containment critical, but not guaranteed. We could not waver or relax in our supervision of Alex.

Sensing that God was teaching me a bigger lesson through the drama with our dog, I prayed for guidance about our ministry with a high-risk, high-profile sexual offender. He was to be released from prison soon and we needed to find a safe place for him where he would be sufficiently supervised.

God told me, "Don't relax out of sympathy for the client ... or because everything looks good ... or because the client says he is much improved."

I drew the connection between the client and our dog. Alex is a friendly creature, my best friend, and always eager to please. However, when presented with the right stimuli she could be triggered into an out-of-control state of destruction. I realized it was probably the same with our client. I had developed a healthy pastoral relationship with him and trusted his good intentions, but needed to bear in mind that he might also be subject to losing control and acting in destructive ways should he encounter an inappropriate or triggering situation.

So I worked with the local law enforcement and community leaders to establish a strong support system with adequate boundaries in which he'd most likely thrive and not hurt anyone—hoping I'd be more successful with the client than Jo and I had been with Alex!

In the end I learned that sometimes God teaches us about our lives in mysterious ways. We just have to learn to connect the dots and make sense of the bigger picture.

This time I succeeded!

Twilight and Short Leash II

3:58 a.m.

God opens my eyes. Blinking to clear my vision, the clock blinks back at me.

4:00 a.m.

The clock displays Chronos time, but God lives in another time not created by man. In His time, known as Kairos, it is time for me to rise up:

> The hour has already come for you to wake up from your slumber, because our salvation is nearer now than when we first believed. The night is nearly over; the day is almost here. So let us put aside the deeds of darkness and put on the armor of light (*Romans 13:11-13*).

I grew up in a dysfunctional alcoholic family with little structure, never knowing what would happen. The church provided respite and sanctuary, sending me to Rockpoint Summer Camp where I would participate as a camper for one week, then work in the kitchen the rest of the season. It was an amazing experience that provided the structure I lacked at home. Meals were on time. Every day had a reliable schedule with work and a variety of fun events. But there was also an ease about things wherein we enjoyed the natural flow of the day. And like most healthy homes, it wasn't too rigid—sometimes I would even sneak out at midnight with other staff and go swimming at North Beach.

Wahoo!

Ever since that summer I have lived according to Chronos time, regulated by the strictures of a demanding world. I entered into ministry through the Kairos Prison Ministry, but am still guided by Chronos time. It has worked, enabling me to pay the bills and keep things running, but it is stressful on those who aren't as dedicated to it as myself. My wife, Pastor Jo, also suffers from my addiction to Chronos. God is calling me through her to grow closer to Him.

Walking into the forest in the twilight of the morning I realize that God is calling me to change over from man-made Chronos time to His time, Kairos. I do this by moving where God tells me to move and doing what God tells me to do in His time, when He says it's time. This is Kairos. It also means allowing others who God puts in my life to guide me through the twilight—especially when I am treading unfamiliar pathways.

❖

Walking with Alex on the "short leash" I realize she is better equipped than I am to navigate the forest in the twilight. In the dimming light after sundown her senses are sharp whereas, in comparison, mine are dull. She smells the leaves of the bushes on the edges of the trail and can tell who walked by and what they were doing and when they were there—maybe even what they last ate. She is like the breeze flowing through the environment, completely contiguous and interrelated with everything. I, on the other end of the "short leash," bumble along trying to keep up …

Shiloh, our cat, trots behind at a safe distance, then with a sudden and impetuous burst of cat energy races across the trail and straight up a tree trunk into its sprawling limbs. Wild-eyed and bushy-tailed, he wastes no time, but immediately leaps back upon the forest floor and races up the trail ahead of us and out of sight.

❖

My furry companions live in another version of this world, one in which time is not a militant sergeant barking orders but rather a carnival of amazements that delight and enchant. Living in Chronos time helps me to monitor them, but they too reveal the beauty of the Kairos by which God is guiding me back to my true nature and unity with Him. For He is all the world and all the time and all that has ever existed. When I fail to trust his infinitely greater wisdom and goodness, whereby I step off my anointed path, I find myself at odds with life. But when I heed His call and am where I am supposed to be according to His time, I find peace within myself and with the world.

Dawn

"As lightning flashes from East to West, so will be the coming of the Son of Man."

Matthew 24:27

As the sky becomes tinged with the light of the closest star, song birds begin to sing and crows caw loudly, announcing the rising Son. The creatures of night become silent in the light, retreating into their hidden places of refuge ... as the leaves on the trees reach upward to grasp the luminescence, their job to fill every available space and soak in the presence of the celestial starshine.

Alex is on the leash, leading me through the forest. Though I am the alpha, her job is to inspect the trail, understand who lurks there beyond my comprehension, deduce the sounds and smells of the landscape for my benefit, and, when confident, lead me from the valley of despair onto higher ground. If I tug too much and interrupt her or impose my will too forcefully upon her instinctive wisdom, I will lose the benefit of knowledge she offers.

Giant trees grow old throughout the terrain, then pass, opening new space for younger trees to flourish. Sometimes new growth saplings will huddle beside an old forest giant for protection and stability. There are areas where there is a community of giants, mature, tall and straight. Yet they all began as seeds that sprouted from the new earth and grew beneath the shelter of those mature trees that came before them.

Each tree reaching for the light, its journey of growth awakened by the dawning sun that returns again and again after every single night.

Embedded Roots

"Your word is a lamp to guide my feet and a light for my path."

Psalms 119:105

There are roots embedded in the forest pathways that sometimes rise above the surface as the ground is traveled upon and worn down. I know they are there, and I know they stick up just to catch the unaware foot or toe when you aren't looking out!

"For he will order his angels to protect you wherever you go. They will hold you up with their hands so you won't even hurt your foot on a stone"

Psalms 91:11,12

Back in the forest again this morning for the second time, I left the walking staff at home and started jogging a little until the asthma kicked in. Ouch! I stubbed my stupid sore toe again. *Lord, why always the sore one?* A lesson to pay attention no matter what you are doing.

Phil Zaldotte said, "Don't break your routine. Perseverance is key, especially with The Lord."

I decided to put on my hiking shoes tonight. I had been wearing sneakers, which are a lot easier to put on and off and are more comfortable. But my daily routine of walking in the forest at night, as directed by The Lord, entailed wearing hiking shoes. According to *Eph.*
6:15, we are to be shod with "the preparation of the Gospel of peace." Putting on the hiking shoes was my way of acknowledging to God that I had been in error by changing the routine of footwear.

No stubbing the toe tonight! Praise God! Lesson learned.

"A prudent person foresees danger and takes precautions. The simpleton goes blindly on and suffers the consequences."

Proverbs 27:12

Wildfires

A mish-mash of fallen tree limbs and torn brambly clumps litter the forest, the result of disastrous winter storms. On the grand scale it is "tinder" ripe for burning. Given the right conditions (drought, lightning, a careless cigarette or, God forbid, an arsonist) it will ignite a wildfire that could quickly devour the woods and surrounding neighborhoods in a conflagration of flames.

In urban areas we see another kind of devastating force that acts like a wildfire when social stressors pitch too high and populations erupt in anger and rebellion. We must take care not to let the debris and detritus of our minds go unchecked, lest they become "triggered" by any offending phenomenon that sends our incendiary emotions into full-fledged assault mode. Like whole forests consumed by fire, our human neighborhoods and cities can be quickly destroyed by rage.

❖

Out there in the forest the Lord showed me our world.

As I enter the forest I notice the tremendous storm damage, tree limbs and debris scattered across the ground. Some trees have been up-rooted by the stormy winds because the roots were shallow, not reaching deep enough in the ground. The fallen trees remind me of Jesus' parable of the seeds falling on rocky soil (*Matt 13:20-21*). Like communities that had great visions but ultimately failed because they lacked the grounding to manifest in a long-lasting manner.

There are trees that are old and very large, but still standing strong and healthy. They seem to congregate in communities with smaller trees growing up around them—like a schoolroom of children learning and being nurtured by the senior trees. Or like devout disciples of Jesus and his magnanimous teachings.

There is another area with groups of large trees, but no smaller trees growing beneath them, not even ferns. The senior trees in these communities soak up all the sunlight so that none of it reaches the ground to nourish new growth.

Do we have leaders like that?

There are also large trees that are dead but still standing. The bark has rotted away, with bits and hunks falling off. Woodpeckers feed on the parasitic insects inside the tree trunk. The life has left and the tree is dead but still standing in the forest.

We have churches like that. Don't we?

Many trees have broken at their weak points because the storm winds became too strong. It reminds me of how people fall into ruin when they succumb to their character flaws.

There are areas where severe winds have pushed a group of trees down all at once into messy clumps, kind of like some communities wherein severe trauma has struck, leaving its members scarred and paralyzed.

There are areas where pretty green ferns have grown up and covered the ground with a beautiful green leafy blanket. But, having seen this before, I know it is merely a camouflage that covers the heaps of dead wood that dwell beneath—the aftermath of storms that wreaked damage—creating a surplus of tinder that makes perfect fuel for a wildfire. We have communities where everything is neat and pretty on the surface, but underneath the camouflage there is damage, pain, anger, and despair.

There is another area where the people living in condos have purged their back yards of the fallen tree brush and limbs from storm-damaged trees by dragging it into the forest. Just on the other side of the back fence you can see huge haphazard piles where the people threw the unseemly sticks, limbs and brush over the fence so they could have a clean, pretty yard.

"NIMBY" (not in my back yard) they say. "We don't want those ugly damaged people in our community. We just want the nice, pretty people like us."

❖

The Lord is showing me that the wildfires will come more frequently. The recent riots in St. Louis demonstrate that the fiery forces of human nature abound as our world is quaking beneath our feet and beginning to rush downward in an avalanche towards the bottom.

Our human communities are damaged from unresolved trauma, unmet needs, financial stress, and ongoing social conflict—and it only takes a spark to set the community on fire.

It is time to search for those souls who can be saved and rescue them from the impending destruction. The earth is quaking under our feet.

It's time to get our eyes on Jesus. He is on the way and we need to be about His business until He arrives.

Benched

In the forest with Alex on leash, we came to a point on the trail where there was a very large pine tree. Many of its limbs had broken off during a snow and ice storm the previous winter—after which I had cleaned up the brambly mess that had frozen onto the trail.

I noticed a newly built park-style bench just off the trail, and thought, "Great! A chance to sit and rest." I walked to the bench and sat down, then noticed a few long sticks that had fallen off the tree above that were leaning against a smaller tree. Having had a career as a mechanical engineer—and a propensity for keeping everything straight, level, square and in its proper place—I got up and grabbed the sticks. Then I noticed a large dead branch caught above me in the small tree. "A widow maker," I thought. Or as my lumberjack father would say, "A dead man."

After directing Alex off to the side where she would be safe, I took the longest stick and poked at the limb to knock it down. Rather than falling cleanly, it broke into pieces, some of which hit me in the head and face. It didn't hurt, but was annoying.

Suddenly I heard, "Peter, get back on the trail."

I tried, but Alex's leash was tangled in a pile of brush and limbs. After untangling the leash, I was finally able to get back to the path.

Then God spoke again, "Peter, stay on the anointed trail I gave you. If you get too caught up in the damaged areas, you will never get back on the trail."

At once the metaphor became crystal clear. There were people I was working with who were so damaged that they would never get free of it. I had to start letting go of those people who were not going to change and were draining our resources and time. And I needed to stay on the trail God anointed me for and let others, who were more qualified than me, go down the side trails I could not.

Blink (Coyotes II)

Blink, blink. My eyes see the glowing clock, blurry until I reach for my glasses.

2:38 a.m. Early shall I rise! The Lord calls!

Last night church at prison was exceptional. The men sat in rapt engagement as I spoke of being led through the dark forest by my dog, facing an impossible situation and crying out to God for help, then receiving instruction from God that enabled me to experience His power and achieve success.

On the way home, I went to *Isaiah 40* and remembered a year before driving down the highway as God gave me visions of the road rising and rippling in large waves, the edges breaking up in pieces of rubble. There were cars in the breakdown lane with their flashers on, yet our car remained level on the highway and had no disturbance.

Jo had been reading *Isaiah 40*:

> Listen it's the voice of someone shouting, "Clear the way through the wilderness for The Lord! Make a straight highway through the wasteland for our God! Fill in the valleys, and level the mountains and hills, straighten the curves, and smooth out the rough places." Then the glory of The Lord will be revealed, and all the people will see it together. The Lord has spoken!

That night in the forest God straightened the pathway and the curves so that I walked straight and ended up on the main path. He did that to emphasize His message from *Isaiah 40*.

The Risen Son is Rising over Vermont!

"As the lightning flashes from the east to the west so shall be the coming of the Son of Man."

Matthew 24:27

Awoken by inner intimations of the coming light, my eyes open to the glowing LED numbers of the clock on the nightstand.
3:45 a.m.

By 4 a.m. I am on the deck with my hot mug of steaming coffee. The sky is becoming light, showing signs of the risen Son coming.

In the dim light of dawn I enter the forest. Coyote cries and howling wolves banter across the terrain, then transform into the low-pitched whistle of a train and cars speeding on the distant highway.

The sky becomes lighter as if God is opening my eyes so I can see more of what He sees.

4:55 a.m.

A hummer does a flyby in back of my head.

Early bird gets the nectar.

The Foundation

"Behold the former things that have come to pass, and new things I declare before they spring forth, I tell you of them."

Isaiah 42:9

God has many things to teach me in the forest. Walking the trails I see old giants that have succumbed to the wind and elements laying quietly on the forest floor. As the years go by moss grows on them. Leaves and other debris fall upon them and create a layer of earthen soil and hummus in which new growth can sprout and begin the cycle again.

A small seed becomes a sapling and eventually sends roots down over the giant and into the ground. As the giant grows older it crumbles and decays, and gradually disintegrates back into the soil on the forest floor, enrichening the growth of future generations. This process of simultaneous decay and regrowth, of death metamorphosing into rebirth, positions the new trees with roots as high as four feet above ground the resulting spectacle is surreal, a tree standing on its finger tips!

But such trees are not properly rooted in the forest floor because they are built on old rotting trees that will continue to decay and dissipate into the ground. Because the new tree is not anchored into the firm foundation of the forest floor it may become unsteady, vulnerable to the forces of nature—gravity, storms, and the creatures that live within the forest that constantly bear down upon all living things.

God showed me that what He wants to do through me is to be a new or unique anointing that will help disciple each person He brings my way into becoming the men and women of God He created them to be.

That anointing must be rooted in the solid truth of the Word of God and by the Spirit of the Lord.

Jesus is the way the truth and the life and light for our paths.

Bloom in Your Garden!

For years whenever a genuine soul has aspired to create their own ministry, I have always heard the fanciful response, "Bloom where you are planted!" In other words, don't wait for an opportunity to unfold in the future, rather, be a representative of Jesus now, where you are in your family, neighborhood, community, workplace and local church.

We all know and believe this as it has been preached to us many times.

But now our social environment and day-to-day situations are changing radically. Turmoil, fear, confusion and control spawned by a pandemic. Violence and mayhem enacted by anarchists and political extremists. Economic devastation and paralysis caused by mass business shutdowns, unemployment and a massive transfer of wealth from the common man to the elites. Excessive government controls and mandates divide the nation. A widespread panic and upheaval with desperate citizens stocking up on household supplies, food, weapons and ammunition. The insanity of social justice radicals calling to defund and abolish the police.

All in all, the world is in a dire and chaotic condition in which we are striving to simply survive the turmoil every day.

Living in such fragmenting times, what are we as Christians to do? What is our personal ministry for the Lord? Is it wise to retreat and hide from the evil that is overwhelming our world? Should we withdraw from social engagement into our homes and hope that God intervenes in time to save us, and our humanity, from further discomfort and danger?

Or are we called to a greater purpose?

Jeremiah was a great prophet speaking for the Lord to a people who had strayed so far from God there was no turning back. And yet He sent Jeremiah to preach and warn them of the coming warfare and destruction of Jerusalem, the exile of survivors in a foreign Land.

Jeremiah was known as the weeping prophet, tasked with a most portentous mission: to speak to a people who would not listen and were doomed. God told Jeremiah, "Do not pray for the well-being of this people." Because He was bringing destruction.

Isaiah had been blessed to prophesy the birth of Jesus. John the Baptist prepared the way for Jesus. But Jeremiah was told to deliver a message that would seemingly redeem no one. It is a test of faith to act when we see no viable beneficial outcome; however, when we are called by the Lord, this is what we must do. Even in the face of despair and desperation, we must continue to walk the path we were made to travel, and do the right thing.

Gods wants each of us who follow Jesus Christ to do so in obedience. Whatever the environment or situation, our purpose remains the same. We are Ambassadors for Christ, bringing the Gospel of Jesus to a lost and hurting world. Wherever we might find ourselves—whether in the CHOP zone of Seattle, under attack by Anarchists, arrested for our Christian beliefs, defending our homes, or moving through a society that is deluded and maligned—our task is to represent Jesus Christ, and not just to those who smile at us and agree with our views, but to everyone we contact.

Life as we know it on the grand scale is changing. Our social and political environments are changing. The mission looks different, but our purpose remains the same.

Keep faith in the Lord and carry on …

The Darkness

Then Jesus asked them, "Would anyone light a lamp and then put it under a basket or under a bed? Of course not! A lamp is placed on a stand, where its light will shine. For everything that is hidden will eventually be brought into the open, and every secret will be brought to light. Anyone with ears to hear should listen and understand."

Mark 4:21-23

Awake at 3:30 a.m.

The forest calls to me in the dark.

Sitting on the deck with Alex, her ears stand up straight as she angles her head and looks fervently into the shadowy woods. An owl hoots and is echoed by another. A strange bird calls out of the darkness, followed by another owl. I imagine a rabbit being stalked from above.

Alex snaps her head to the right, sensing something on the move in the forest. Maybe a bear at the all-you-can-eat buffet of bird feeders in the back yards that skirt the edge of the forest.

Much happens in the dark.

Sitting in the light from the house, Alex and I sense the activities unfolding in the darkness, but are not affected because we are still in the light.

Just as The Spirit of the Living God that lives inside all who believe in Jesus as Savior and Lord reveals truth and discerns evil, the light from our home protects us from the darkness. Just as the Word of God gives us guidance in this world, our familiarity of the forest and those that lurk there gives us wisdom when we enter into that world.

Just as the Word of God illuminates the unknown within us and replaces it with clarity, our light infiltrates the darkness and it is diminished.

Morning

"The faithful love of the Lord never ends! His mercies never cease. Great is his faithfulness; his mercies begin afresh each morning"

Lamentations 3:22-23.

2:58 a.m.

Eyes open. Time to get up and seek the Lord. "Come out on the deck for a while," The Lord says to me.

3:58 a.m.

Out with Shiloh, our Maine Coon rescue cat, wandering around the garden, the first robin is chirping alongside distant rumblings of the early morning commuter traffic. Dull thuds echo from nearby homes. Gun-fire from the ATF director next door? Or a big hammer hitting something? Are those crickets or just the constant ringing in my ears?

4:00 a.m.

The night sky is slowly being infiltrated with glorious light.

4:08 a.m.

Another bird is chirping. A chorus of birdsong reverberates throughout the sky. They are announcing the rising of the Son in the East.
    Darkness flees before the light.

Joshua 1:9

"This is my command—be strong and courageous! Do not be afraid or discouraged. For the Lord your God is with you wherever you go."

Donald (a spiritual son) and I were embarking upon a night walk in the wintertime woods. With recent storms of ice and snow the forest was an icy wonderland of spectacular sights as small trees were bent over with their tops frozen into the ground.

Walking through the gateway into the forest we heard a sudden crack! and crash! as a towering branch splintered off the top of the big pine tree in front of us. Donald quickly leapt backwards and I stepped to the right just as the large limb hit the ground exactly where we had been standing.

Looking at me with trepidation, Donald thought we should return home immediately because it was too dangerous to be in the woods. But remembering Joshua, wherein the Lord has told me I need not fear when following His direction, I stepped over the limb and said, "Let's go on with our walk."

And so we did, without any further problem.

Praise God!

Focus on God

"Thy Word is a lamp unto my feet and a light unto my path."

Psalm 119:105

The grounds surrounding our home have been cleared of forest trash and wreckage. Old logs cut up into 24 inch chunks and stacked like cordwood provide a protective wall, a heavy wooden barrier between our backyard and the forest. We live in a clean, peaceful sanctuary where we can rest, be refreshed, plan, gather, and study before going beyond the wall and into the world.

This night God has called me out into the forest. At this late hour I fear how perilous and foreboding the world can be, and I pray. God assures me that I will be safe and sound as long as I stay on the anointed path He has placed me on.

Walking the woodsy trail with Alex, I see a little flash in my headlight as something sparkling descends on a silken thread from the canopy. I try to focus on it and lose my balance, stumbling a bit before I find my footing back on the path.

As we progress on the trail that loops through the forest and are returning home, I see a pair of glowing eyes about 15 feet high in a tree. I stare at this strange and mesmerizing creature for several minutes, adjusting my head lamp and closing in to get a better view. When my attention returns to the path I realize Alex has slipped away, quietly, into the darkness. Then I realize that all the while, in the back of my mind, I had heard God telling me, "Peter, you are being distracted." But, like a child, fascinated by the mysterious eyes of the nocturnal creature, I chose not to listen.

Was it an owl? A raccoon?

"Peter, you are being distracted."

I turn back to right myself on the path and am ensnared in a tangle of small saplings and leaves pointing in all directions. All at once I'm lost and don't know where the trail is. Distressed, I direct the luminescence of my headlight through the underbrush and find the path again.

To find Alex I must leave the anointed path and go to Starbird Road, where my instincts tell me she has fled and is waiting. Ten minutes later I find her, acting guilty, for even she, my trusted canine companion, knows that we have diverged from the anointed path God intended us to walk.

Our brief expedition in the woods this night revealed more than a rejuvenation with nature, it imparted an important lesson. God showed me how my tendency towards distraction causes problems, potentially wasting time and the precious moments I am given to walk a path of purpose. This time the stakes weren't too high, just a confused dog who anxiously strayed from her master—in much the same way that I strayed from God's focus on the anointed path. But next time could be different. Next time the stakes for becoming distracted could be a lost life or a missed opportunity to stop a crime or a failure to provide help for someone in need.

In His mercy God is preparing me for my life as an emissary of His good will, holding the sacred mantle of Pastor, and assuming responsibility for helping my fellow man find and trust Him. To do this I need to stay focused on the path He has set out for me, listening to God's guidance and following Him at every step along the way—even in the dark midnight wilderness walking with the dog just beyond the sanctuary of my safe home.

Three Trees

"Though one may be overpowered by another, two can withstand him.
And a threefold cord is not quickly broken"

Eccl 4:12

Walking with Alex and Shiloh in the forest at daybreak. A big week ahead with important decisions that Jo and I must confer with the Lord to make. "Lord keep us within Your will. Do not let us be misled or distracted from the pathway you have us on."

Then I saw a tree I had never noticed. It was actually three trees wrapped around each other. Then I saw three trees that had not wrapped around each other. How much stronger is the stand of three!

In the Valley

My walks in the forest have grown quiet, the time of intense fellowship and communication with the Lord come to an end. Is the training done? The teaching over? It was fantastic while it was happening. I felt powerful, confident, strong, and excited. Now, back to normal life again, I feel sad.

Why Lord?

"Peter, you live and work in the valley, not the mountain top."

He was right. Everything in my life, including lessons from the forest, was to prepare us for living and working in the valley.

But God said, "Listen! It's the voice of someone shouting, 'Clear the way through the wilderness for the Lord! Make a straight highway through the wasteland for our God! Fill in the valleys, and level the mountains and hills. Straighten the curves, and smooth out the rough places. Then the glory of the Lord will be revealed, and all people will see it together. The Lord has spoken!" (*Isaiah 40:3-5*).

He will be with us in the Valley!

Praise God!

V.

CHURCH AT PRISON:
STORIES BY & ABOUT INMATES

Church at Prison Poem

Inevitably, without intervention, by those showing the love of God:

A baby is born into a broken world.
A child is mentally and spiritually damaged by abuse and neglect.

A teenager decides to never be controlled and hurt again.
A life becomes controlled by inner anger, rage and pain.

A line is drawn by state and federal laws.
A line is crossed.

A law is broken.
A crime is defined.

A "perp" is arrested and the storm begins.
The "perp" is booked and the dark clouds form.

A file is started and a new history with incarceration begins.
A court arraignment is recorded.

A storm rolls in and, with new history, expands and intensifies.
The storm clouds darken with strong winds, thunder and lightning.

Everything is swept away by the storm; the old life, family, friends, possessions, occupation and reputation.

Horrible damage and pain is inflicted.
We see the "perp," God sees a generation of children

damaged, lost and hurt.
Life in prison begins: wounded, broken, hopeless, depressed,

discouraged, with the lights out in the dark cell the "perp" calls out to a God he does not know, desperately hoping God is real and hears

his cries of anger and pain.
God hears the prayer by the child He created in the womb.

"God if you are there I need your help. PLEASE be there for me."
God reaches down into the dark storm and grabs the hand of the

forsaken.
"I Am!"

Time goes by—days, weeks, months, even years—before the "perp" gets his or her day in court. Innocent until proven guilty.

Life in prison is by the convict code "Survival of the fittest,
like it had been on the street!

A Bible is given, opened and a light pierces the darkness.
The broken child goes to "church at prison" and hears that his or her

name is not shame or "perp," but "Beloved child of God."
A new life is born as the broken child accepts the grace and mercy

of Jesus Christ on the cross. Repentance, baby steps, forgiveness, and healing ensue....

Patmos Christian College

January-February, 2000 Newsletter
Update from the Registrar, Richard Kidson

In the July-Sept, '99 issue of this Newsletter you read how the Church at Prison had entered into a covenant with VISION International University of Ramona, California to become an affiliate college. We are excited to be able to report to you the following:

January 2000 witnessed the start of accredited college classes offered by Patmos Christian College at the Northwest State Correctional Facility in St. Albans, Vermont. It is our view that this was God's answer to prophetic words that Our Lord would raise up men from behind the walls who would be attuned to the current move of the living God in our day. Men who have received the vision of a 'great awakening' by God in our land have heard the commission: "Go, and tell the people," and they have responded like Isaiah, "Lord, here I am, send me" (*Isaiah 6:8*).

Patmos is a small volcanic island, serving, along with other Aegean islands, as a penal isle where the apostle John was exiled for speaking about God and bearing witness to Jesus. (Re 1:9) While there, he received "the Revelation of Jesus Christ," by which the last book of the Bible is so named. Therefore, when this new affiliate college was looking for a name by which to be recognized for the purpose of accreditation, combined with the fact that the first classes of this college would be offered inside a correctional facility, we were led by the Spirit that Patmos Christian College would be the most fitting name.

It is the belief of Patmos Christian College that all who are called unto Christ are to be conformed to His image. This is not an instantaneous event, but a discipleship process. Therefore, we are set up, as many other ministries, to effectively train, certify and release men and women of God to reach our world with the Gospel of Jesus Christ. Our program is rich in spiritual content, Biblical study, and ministry training. In other words, because we all have received various "gifts" from God and been called to a specific service within His grand universal plan, the goal of Patmos Christian College is to raise up and develop workers, shepherds, prayer warriors and teachers for His ministry in the 21st century.

Our first semester began with four (3-credit) courses being offered:

1. Hermeneutics: How to Study the Bible
2. Old Testament Survey
3. New Testament Survey
4. Marriage and Family Life

All classes during the first semester averaged between 10 and 13 registered students, meeting for 13 weeks once a week for 2½ hours of lecture and classroom discussion. A total of 30 credits (10 courses, 3 credits each) will earn a student within the first year of studies a Certificate in Biblical Studies. These credits may be applied to the 2nd year of studies (11 courses, 33 credits) to earn an associate degree in biblical studies. This program will allow students to advance towards a Bachelor of Arts Degree in Theological Studies, Christian Counseling, Christian Education, International Relations, or Christian business Management (120 total credits needed for this Degree).

The aforementioned is not a comprehensive statement of all the goals and objectives, nor all the specifics, of what Patmos Christian College intends to do as it moves alongside the will of God in our lives.

All of us, as born-again, spirit-filled Christians must begin to see as our Lord does and have His vision that "the earth be filled with the Knowledge of the Glory of the Lord, as the waters cover the sea" (*Hab 2:14*).

Addendum: Support Needed - Patmos College

We are now ordering textbook masters for our 2nd semester. Donations are needed to cover registration ($10 per student each semester) and textbooks ($10-$15 per student for each course taken).

Some students are working towards a degree that will prepare them for a career in Ministry. Other students are taking courses to better equip them for Christian life inside and after release. Some are curious and are "sitting in" (auditing). Of 23 students who signed up, 18 are sticking with it in the fourth week.

Pastor Pete

Church At Prison

*Serving The Men and Women Affected by Incarceration
and Their Families since 1992*

Sean Allain's Story

My name is Sean Allain. When I was arrested in 1990, I believed my life was over. After my arrest, I was a real mess and the way I lived my life displayed just that. I refused to clear up my court proceedings for over four years because I feared what the future held for me.

Looking back now, I can see my problems started before I was six years old, but they really got worse when I was placed into the custody of the state at the age of six. I was state-raised you might say, and as I reflect on my early years in state's custody I can see it as the beginning of my life sentence that I am now serving as an adult in prison.

I did many stupid things while I waited on a deal to cross my path that would give me any type of hope at leaving prison.

D Wing – Close Custody Unit

With tears of pain and sorrow, Sean Allain shared his story with me in the laundry room in D Wing Close Custody unit.

Sean had experienced abuse from his mother's male and female lovers. Then, after being placed in VT Foster care, he experienced more abuse. Finally, Sean ended up in the VT Juvenile Detention Center in Essex Junction. As he approached the age of 18 he was told that he would be released from state custody. That was the law!

Sean pleaded with his case workers to not release him. He wasn't ready to be thrown out into the world on his own. He told them, "If you release me I'm going to kill someone." But he had to be released and he was.

Now in 1993, he wanted to stop hurting people and causing pain with all the legal games he had been playing to delay his trial. We prayed together and he gave his life to the Lord Jesus.

God gave me *1 Corinthians 13:11* to share with him. "When I was a child I spoke as a child, I understood as a child; but when I became a man, I put away childish things." This seemed to be a powerful message that said, "It's time to grow up and, for whatever is left of your life, begin to do things correctly." The time came for the games and delays to stop and a plea bargain was agreed upon that would bring the process of nearly four years to an end for everyone.

My spirit was riding high when I arrived home that night. The experience of God giving me a scripture to minister to Sean, a man charged with a double murder, was exhilarating. I turned on the TV and was shocked to see a report on Sean and details of his crime. It was horrendous. My human brain could not handle the difference between what I experienced in the D Wing laundry Room and the report on the news. My mind was in a state of turmoil and I was unable to sleep for hours.

How could God give me such a wonderful experience and then show me the brutal crime committed?

"For My thoughts *are* not your thoughts, Nor *are* your ways My ways," says the LORD.

"For *as* the heavens are higher than the earth, So are My ways higher than your ways, And My thoughts than your thoughts"

Isaiah 55:8-9

The Sentence

I arrived early to the court in Bennington, VT and was given permission by the Sheriff's Deputy, who knew me, to meet with Sean before the sentencing hearing. We prayed and God gave me a scripture for him. *2 Corinthians 5:17:* "Therefore if any man is in Christ, he is a new creature: old things have passed away; behold, all things have become new." The message was that Sean was a new child of God and not the old person he had been. The justice system and society sees the criminal requiring a sentence that fits the crime. God, who is in control of everything, sees his child clothed in the white robes of righteousness.

During the proceedings a relative of a victim spoke to the judge concerning her opinion of the sentence that should be imposed. During her statement she referred to him as "that creature." She was thinking of the "creature-murderer," not knowing that he was a "new creature in Christ."

God had prepared a word before the hearing, knowing that these words were coming.

Before the judgement Sean was allowed to speak to the court and said that he hoped someday in the years to come that the relatives of the victims would somehow be able to forgive him. How easy it is for God to forgive us when we sincerely ask! How difficult it is for human beings to forgive each other and give up the traumatic pain from a brutal crime. How easy it is to be captured by hatred, unforgiveness, and bitterness when someone has injured our lives.

The moment a prisoner accepts Jesus Christ as Lord and Savior he becomes a citizen of the Kingdom of Heaven.

When Jesus was hanging on the cross and the thief acknowledged Him as Lord and Savior, Jesus told him, "Surely this day you will be with me in Paradise." He died a "New creature in Christ" while the justice system carried out its punishment on him for being a thief. He joined Jesus in paradise, but did the soldiers, High Priest or Pontius Pilot join Jesus in paradise when they died?

Maybe they did and maybe they didn't.

How significant it is that Jesus chose a convict being executed to be the first person in Paradise after His death. The man had no time to be baptized, confirmed, read the Bible, go to church, or any other normal act of righteousness. The idea that a criminal can be forgiven by God for a crime while a victim is captured by hate and unforgiveness is more than most human minds can comprehend.

If I was God I would have picked a nice person, such as Billy Graham or Mother Theresa, to be the example and first person in.

But, I thank God that I have been forgiven for what I have done. I want to follow the God that forgave the thief on the cross. Left up to the forgiveness of other human beings, would any of us make it?

Having a justice system and a Department of Corrections is a good thing. Our system was patterned after God's design in the Bible.

In the Kingdom of Heaven we have forgiveness and total pardon. That's where I put my faith and hope for the future. Amen! In our prayers for men in prisons we need to remember to also pray for victims that have been hurt. Ask God to heal their wounds and release them from any unforgiveness and bitterness that has captured them.

by Pastor Pete (authorized by Sean Allain)

The Release

As Pastor Fred and I prayed for Leo, he began to weep. He was scared to be released into a society that hated him and would consider him to be a high-risk sex offender. His picture and information would be on the internet. The media would seek to sensationalize his release, inflame the public opinion against him and enforce civil confinement, whether it applied to him or not.

Working with DOC we were able to develop an out-of-state relocation plan for Leo, but as the date for release approached his anxiety level increased. The night before release he buried his head in Pastor Fred's shoulder and cried. He hated prison, but also hated leaving close friends behind. Prison is an environment you hate, but you also love parts of it, such as the friends you make and the familiarity you forge. It is a curse that God turns into blessing for some. It is bad but good, evil but holy, of the Devil but invaded by God. It is needed and serves Vermont well—better than most states!

On the morning of release Leo walked out of the booking door towards my car. A caseworker walking down the sidewalk on his way in to work gave him a big smile, a hug and a pat on the back. As we drove away and the distance from the prison increased, I could see him relaxing from 10 years of incarceration as waves of emotion filled his eyes with tears.

At our home Leo settled into his room and unpacked the two boxes containing his possessions. Later, while watching a movie on the TV, he got up, went to his room and shut the door. Back at the prison it was headcount time. Each day all inmates would be locked in their cells until headcount was secured.

"Whoops! I'm not in prison anymore!" Leo remembered, then returned to watch the movie with a little smile of embarrassment.

His Prisoner's Rights advocate dropped by for a short visit to say goodbye and encourage him in his new life. Later that evening his sister came to have dinner with him, bearing hugs, tears, and promises to stay in touch. Our agent in the other state called to say hello and give Leo final instructions on getting from the airport to his room. As they talked his anxiety diminished with the assurance that there is at least one person in the new location who will be glad to see him and will receive him as a brother.

The next morning he said goodbye Vermont. There was a family reunion and dinner waiting in another state where he was to meet with another sister, a brother and his mother. For the first time in many years he spent time with his family as a free man. After many tears and much laughter, the trip continued through a few more states until we arrived at a hotel for the night. In the morning we said goodbye as he boarded his plane for his final destination and new life.

For the next week we received several calls updating us on his quest for a new life. He contended with the sex offender registration in the new state, a job fair where he applied for at least one job, and several days of job hunting. Finally he was hired by a restaurant—which is very common for ex-convicts. Look around the next time you eat out and you may see our clients cooking, washing dishes, even waiting on tables!

Without The Church At Prison working with Vermont DOC and State Police, Leo would have been released into the public with community notification, leading to another media circus that would drive him out of wherever he tried to live and away from any chance of a stable life and employment. Which is entirely counterproductive—being homeless, jobless, and at odds with society increases the risk of new crimes and more victims. But this time God showed favor and provided a new life for His child!

Letter to Bob Sawyer from Agnes Fiske

Dear Bob,

Two weeks ago I felt moved to write to you, but did not. Please forgive me because I believe it was the Holy Spirit telling me. I have a sense that you are very sad and depressed. Well, my brother, it must be very difficult for you right now. I am praying for you, and if and when you want to talk please call us. One of the many things that I have learned since October is that we need to allow people to feel the way they do!

Some Christians try to talk people out of feeling the way they do and, therefore, deny their feelings. HOGWASH! We need to listen to people's hearts and then talk if they want us to. Sometimes we just need to listen, and other times we need to listen and speak life into situations.

I am typing this because I had an operation last week. After Chemotherapy, my tumor shrunk 80%, which is great. The last few weeks of chemo was quite a trip, let me tell you. I will share that some other time. I was to start radiation treatments for six weeks, five days a week. After the Tumor Board met to discuss my case, they advised me to have surgery to remove the rest of the tumor and any living cancer cells that still existed, and then have radiation. I got real bummed out over the fact that my surgeon would not do it, but then ended up with a specialist.

God does know what He is doing!!! He took 17 lymph nodes out; six had dead cancer cells in them, six had living cancer cells, and the rest were cancer free. It was a God thing that I had the surgery. I went to have my drain taken out today, but now have to wait until Monday because too much is still draining. Oh well! Next Tuesday I go to Dr. Rueben to set up radiation. The doctors have been great, very honest and straight forward. Thank You, Lord. Today there is physical pain, but it lessens every day.

My hair is now one inch long and I do not wear my wig. My son, Nathan, and Pastor Duane encouraged me with that, even though Duane didn't know how much I disliked wearing it! For one week I have NOT been able to do ANYTHING!!! Stir crazy has been the word!!! Sunday afternoon I watched two Westerns in a row. I could get hooked on those!!! *King of Texas*, then *Wyatt Earp*. The Earps were all classy looking in this one!!!

I have many testimonies to share with you, but I will do just one for now. On April 10th, Pete and I were laying in bed talking and he asked me how I was feeling. I said, "Wonderful," and he asked me why. Without even thinking about it, I said, "Because I like myself." What a revelation!!! I said, "I am 56 years old, and for the first time in my life I like myself." But it has nothing to do with me—IT IS GOD!!! *Psalm 139:14* became so very real to me: "I WILL PRAISE YOU, FOR I AM FEARFULLY AND WONDERFULLY MADE; MARVELOUS ARE YOUR WORKS, AND THAT MY SOUL KNOWS VERY WELL."

Isn't that great!?!?!? What a time in a woman's life to feel that way. I have one breast. At the time I had NO hair. My eyebrows and lashes fell out, and some of my fingernails had fallen off. My skin looked like that of a 100 year old woman, having changed from yellow to white from the chemotherapy drugs. According to worldly and even most Christian woman's standards, it was not a good time to feel good about yourself, and look at what God did!!! When I said that, the Holy Spirit gave me POWER!!! The power of KNOWING I could do ANYTHING that was put to me under ANY CIRCUMSTANCE!!!

Hallelujah!!!

Since that night, I have ministered and been in situations that I would always shy away from. Thank You, Lord!!! This is only one of the many things that I will share with you, my brother.

Read and think on *Psalm 139:14* for yourself, brother! God's Word says that "YOU ARE FEARFULLY AND WONDERFULLY MADE, AND MARVELOUS ARE HIS WORKS." It matters not what man nor woman says about us, it is what God says. Since April 10th, I have been free from human condemnation or disapproval. The following Sunday I shared this during testimony time, then came back to my seat and opened my Bible right to the pages where I had stuck my mom's newspaper obituary. I said to myself, "Yes, free at last." You know that I was very displeasing to my mom—how I looked and acted, and certainly being in prison ministry, etc.

I do hope that I have not bored you with all of this. You know that you are a very special brother in my life. Well, the weather here is hot and we are supposed to have a storm tonight. Not my favorite kind, of course!!! Peter is at the facility right now doing a newcomers course. I was supposed to go with him, but obviously did not.

Please write and/or call and let us know how you are. We do love and care about you.

I hit something on the computer that gave me a capital letter at the beginning of some of my sentences!!! I will never understand these machines and probably do not want to!

Inside, On The Way Outside

by James Rivers

After 12 long years of being locked inside the Chittenden County Correctional Center, Jay is now anxiously awaiting a momentous occasion—a "day pass to the world-at-large." Chaperoned by Pastors Pete and Agnes, Jay will enjoy his first "freedom meal" in over a decade—in which *he* gets to choose what to eat instead the jailhouse lunch lady! If Jay does well on this outing and continues to progress towards his release goals, he will eventually be let go from confinement altogether, which makes this a sort of "test run for freedom."

What's it like to be released into the world after having lived in captivity for so long?

Although there is a tremendous amount of anticipation, ironically, the most common emotion is fear. When a man is deprived of the freedom to make decisions and interact with the world in a voluntary way, he is also relinquished of the responsibility to be a productive person. And just as a broken limb in a cast will begin to whither and atrophy, when one is locked up, so does the capacity to cope with the challenges of living as an adult in a difficult world.

Although Jay is now a grown man, in some way rejoining life-at-large after having been confined for many years is like a child getting on the school bus for the first time—his parents have told him about school for a year and he's been getting increasingly excited, but when the time comes it's frightening to actually go.

Paradoxically, the utter lack of freedom inflicted in incarceration is accompanied by a huge amount of security and regularity. Although it is essentially an imposition, everything you need to physically survive—shelter, food, clothing—is provided for you. Meals are served at the same time and periods of work and recreation scheduled uniformly day-to-day. You grow to understand the workings of living in prison and eventually master it. You survive because you know the rules, yet you desire freedom and another chance to live on your own again.

All the time you are locked up you think about being out. But when the fruit of your hard work and aspiration finally arrives—freedom at last!—you have to let go of the security of what you know to walk back into the unknown again.

The world ...

After 12 long years of incarceration Jay has thought a lot about life in the free world. He wonders how much things have changed and if he will be ready for it all. Will the "normal people" be able to tell that he's been in jail? Will they accept him? When he is finally freed for good, what is he going to do. How should he act and where should he go? Will he find a good job? How will he adapt? It feels overwhelming because he has so much to learn.

Thankful to God for a chance to taste freedom, Jay never thought he would make it this far: an opportunity for a new start. With so much he wants to do, Jay feels cautious and knows he's got to take it slow. It's been so long since he's been outside the prison walls, sitting and waiting for the pastors he wonders if it is really going to happen. For someone who's never lost their freedom this may sound strange, but for someone who has been locked up for years in a concrete building with a small yard enclosed with barbed wire fence, the prospect of freedom is mind-blowing.

Although this is just a day trip into the free world, Jay knows that his ultimate freedom is just a short time away—as long as he stays on the prudent path. It's a good reminder to be diligent in changing his attitude and lifestyle to be positive and productive.

After being in jail for the past 12 years he wants to prove to himself that he can make it out there. He'd like to appreciate all the things he lost while enjoying what little he has. There are many things Jay needs to change about himself. For so many years he's felt like a caged animal, but now he has a chance to regain a sense of dignity in his life, a chance to improve himself and realize his dreams of a new life.

Waiting for his pastors to arrive at the jail, Jay keeps telling himself that everything will be ok and that it's no big deal. But he knows when he walks through the doors to the outside world he'll be more than scared. And he'll carry the memories of a lot of hard times as a reminder.

All in all, he thinks the hardest part of being free again will be trying to explain what he's been through—because if you've never had to do time, you'll never understand it.

❖

At long last, Pastors Pete and Agnes arrive to escort Jay into the world-at-large—something they enjoy immensely as a process of liberating the men and women they worked with from a state of imprisonment into freedom.

"Well, here we go! I can handle this," Jay exclaims to Pastor Pete as they walk him out of the prison and into the parking lot to their car. "This is weird!" he says with a smile as they duck inside the car to leave. As they drive to one of Pastor Pete and Agnes's favorite restaurants, The Boathouse, Jay is awed by how big and sprawling the world is. Encountering a free and open society is almost surreal, like revisiting a place where he lived a long time ago. As they arrive at the restaurant, he hopes he won't make a fool of himself.

Jay walks up to the door, folds his arms and waits for the control room officer to click open the door. No click! No control room officer watching the door! Pastor Pete reaches for the door and opens it for Jay. Not sure how to behave, Jay decides to follow his chaperones and just sort of do what they do. It all feels very strange, but also very good.

A tad self-conscious, Jay hopes no one knows he is on a day-pass from prison. Although the average person never stops to think about it, being convicted of a crime and then incarcerated tends to be more than a humbling experience, it's a major blow to one's self-esteem after which one must learn how to act like a free person again. This is accomplished by taking accountability and making amends for one's poor decisions and bad actions. And it works. When we do good things and turn our lives around, we tend to feel better about ourselves and are more likely to treat others well and thrive in society.

Jay enjoys eating without being watched by correctional officers and revels in a freshly cooked meal. The food smells and tastes great—the best meal he's had for a long, long time! After lunch they walk around town and Jay is impressed by how much nice stuff there is—clothing, artwork and galleries, snack shops where you can get whatever you want to eat, fancy buildings, nicely dressed people, pretty women, well-manicured parks and stately statues—so much beauty in the world. (Although he is a bit shocked by how much everything costs!) The greatness of it all makes Jay more hopeful to get out of jail for good so he can get a job and enjoy being a regular citizen who buys his own clothes and enjoys all that society has to offer.

Having enjoyed an experience of freedom, Jay doesn't want the day to end. "How am I going to handle going back to the jail?" he asks Pastor Agnes. She reminds him that he is working towards being released for good and that she and Pastor Pete will help him arrive at the final goal.

"Don't worry about it now. Just enjoy everything," she encourages him.

As they drive back to the Chittenden County Correctional Center, Jay laments that the day has gone by so fast. "I can't wait until I'm free again!" he says. "Thank you Pastors Pete and Agnes! You've been great friends to me, and may God bless you both."

Walking back into his confinement, Jay feels the glum aura of prison. But, at the same time, he has a renewed spark of hope in his heart that there is a better world towards which he is striving and will achieve before too long. He now has something to work towards and a new sense of possibility in his life.

We're rooting for Jay to be free ...

Life Inside Prison for a Christian Inmate

by Bob Sawyer

For the first time since its inception, part of the annual Church At Prison Conference for 1998 was held behind the fence of the Northwest State Correctional Facility on Friday, May 1. That meant church members who live here had the opportunity to participate and serve. Pastor Pete handed out assignments.

I was asked to present a short talk on what life inside here is like for incarcerated Christians seeking the Lord. Several times I sat down and tried to put words on paper; an outline, basic draft, anything at all to prompt me as I stood before the audience in the gym (which included the Superintendent, the Chief Of Security, and Christians leaders from around the state). Nothing would come. Thoughts ran through my mind and a mental outline was taking shape, but I couldn't seem to write them down. I was eventually led to *Luke 21:14-15* which reminds us that the Holy Spirit will provide the words if we stand in faith. So, I decided to test the Word and, on that Friday, stood before the assembled multitude and let Spirit speak through me.

Roughly speaking, this is what I said:

"There is much to do inside the fence here at Northwest. One can work in one of the shops and even make strides toward learning a trade in printing, auto mechanics, or woodworking. There are also basic tasks that pay, such as laundry, floor cleaning, and sewing. If you like to be outside, you can work in the garden or on the grounds crews, which offer a 7-day-a-week occupation. If you seek education, the Silva Education Center offers classes in math, history, grammar, biology, poetry, and art.

"Yes, there are things to do at Northwest.

"The Lord also has much to offer. We have a full-time, in-house Church, pastored by Pete and Agnes Fiske. Services are held every Sunday evening, and Bible studies are scheduled four nights a week. There are ministries in music, intercessory prayer and deliverance. One-on-one counseling is available and so is transition help for those leaving the facility to rejoin life on the outside. The Lord teaches those of us willing to listen that He is no respecter of fences, walls, locked doors, and long sentences. We know from His Word that we are all one body, whether inside or outside the razor wire, and that we can look forward to a peaceful and productive life on either side, and a glorious future with Him when the time comes. And, friends, we all know that time is coming soon.

"Sometimes when folks come to visit, they ask me what they can do. They usually mean they want to buy something for me, to provide something tangible. I like to tell them what I'm going to tell you this afternoon. I ask that they let the outside world know that the body of Christ is alive and well in here. Tell them there is a remnant seeking God's face, who have repented of the sins that put them in here and who have asked the Creator to help them stay free in Him so that there will be no further need for incarceration. Tell them that life goes on for those in the Lord.

"Satan's press wants the public to be afraid of us. The secular media focus on what terrible things have been done by those of us living here hidden and out of view. The public does not know the whole story. You can help. The Lord needs you, we need you, to help balance the record.

"Please tell the world that Christ lives in prison. Please tell the prayer warriors in your community to lift up inmates in their regular prayers. Lives have changed in this facility and places like it all over the world. Please tell people about it. You will be blessed for your efforts."

Fleabag

by Fleabag (with Norman, Birger, and Pastor Pete)

My name is Fleabag. I'm a cat. I used to live in a home where I allowed the people to feed and pet me. But there was no adventure there, so I decided to change the course of my life.

Eventually, while tracking some birds, I crawled under this awesome looking double fence that surrounded a large home where lots of men lived. The sign said "Northwest State Correctional Facility. Authorized persons only!"

Obviously, they knew I was authorized *and* important because the men there greeted me like an old, long lost friend. I spent my first two weeks on a roof. Then a man by the name of Dick said he had a job opening that was right up my alley (not that I am to be confused with an "Alley Cat"!). Free room and board, plus all the mice I could eat. He showed me my new home and called it "The Wood Shop."

In The Wood Shop I adopted several human pets, and one big pet named Birger. Birger had a pet mouse named Bold-D-Guard who was as big as a rat! Without my knowing it, I owed a debt of gratitude to Bold-D-Guard because my job opening had become available after he ate the Boss' beef jerky. But not knowing that Bold-D-Guard was Birger's pet, I immediately had a showdown with him. Of course, the mouse lost, which made Birger very sad, but eventually he got over it.

At times many of my new human pets were nuisances—because I had to be a counselor, a friend, and a good listener. The truth is I helped train Pastor Pete. Afterwards, he showed his appreciation by lightening my work load a bit. But, to be honest, I really didn't mind all the long hours—I put up with the men for their own sake. After all, they had given me a home.

Birger became one of my biggest clients, and I could always count on him to bring me what he called "sewer trout" when he worked on Saturday. He also brought me ham, roast beef, turkey, and seagull—I could have sworn that it tasted like chicken. One day I decided to go after a seagull myself. I almost got him, but then the whole seagull herd came after me. It was a good thing some of my pets came and saved me.

Then things got worse!

With all the good food, my gut got huge. The Boss, who thought I was pregnant or had worms, force-fed me some terrible tasting deworming medicine. I soon lost the big gut (so would you if you swallowed that medicine), but some of the men insisted I had been pregnant and had a miscarriage. Well that upset my pet Birger who thought it was cruel to deworm a pregnant cat. Birger decided I should get "FIXED" so I wouldn't have to suffer through all that again. He gathered donations from several people, and my pet Jay tricked me into a cage.

Then the Boss took me on a trip to a place called the "VETS"! I tried to tell him that this was not in my job description and that I wanted to resign. For over two hours I tried to reason with him, but he wouldn't listen because he was the Boss and I was just an employee! I even threatened him with retribution.

Nothing worked.

When I arrived at the VETS I even tried to argue with Dr. Larrow, but he gave me a sleepy shot, put me on a table and said something about fixing me. That jogged my memory to another time that I had been in a similar place. Suddenly, I had a weird feeling that I had been through this before.

Dr. Larrow started checking me out and laughed. Then he exclaimed, "We can't fix this cat! It's a male and has already been fixed!"

You should have been there to see the ribbing the Boss got from Dr. Larrow. On the way back I told the Boss just what I thought of the whole ordeal. Then I didn't talk to him for over a week.

Poor Birger!

He was shocked when they brought me back. At least it was cheaper than expected. He gave all the donations back, minus the cost of a check-up, the sleepy shot, and a couple shots for safe measure. I later heard rumors that Birger made a profit on the whole deal, but I don't really believe it. I still can't figure out why a bunch of men that can make beautiful oak furniture in that shop can't tell the difference between a female cat and a Tom cat (Tom is a technical term for male among us cats).

I haven't seen my pet Birger lately. He must be on vacation or something. Someone said he went to a "Farm"—but I can't see him milking cows if he can't figure out cats. Anyway, I continue to allow these sweet guys to pet and feed me. They have been known to order special dinners for me, a pound of fresh catfish and cans of tuna.

Recently, I took a tour of the inside of a building where they have a control room and I could smell food cooking. The man in charge assigned another man called "Float" to show me how to get back outside.

The only thing I can't understand now is why they all talk about wanting to leave this place. I think it is a great place to live. Anyway, I've got a great life here and I invite you all to come visit. Feel free to use my name—just say "FLEABAG invited me!"

Reprinted from *The Church at Northwest Newsletter*, July, 1994

The Death of Fleabag

by Bob Sawyer

A much-loved member of the NWSCF community passed away on March 13, 1997. Fleabag the cat, who has been living here for nine years, but who was actually close to twenty years old (very old for a cat), had to be put to sleep by a local vet.

According to Volunteer Coordinator Jerri Brouilette, Fleabag's liver failed him and she and the Vet felt his time had come. Jerri had actually taken the sick animal to the Vet several months ago because of cataracts in his eyes and the liver problem was diagnosed at that time. Thus, while a sad occasion to be sure, most honest observers had to admit that the death was not a surprise.

To say that Fleabag was loved by everyone here, staff and resident alike, is not an exaggeration. For men who have been separated from society, Fleabag provided a rare kind of comfort. Just seeing him sunning on a hot afternoon, or chasing a seagull in the early evening, could bring a smile. He was well-fed, thoroughly indulged with affection, and fiercely protected by one and all. I doubt that anyone making a nasty remark about that cat would fail to hear about it in no uncertain terms. And I know there are many men now back in society who recall Fleabag as one of the positive factors of life here.

Those who grieve his passing should remember that Fleabag was loved, and he knew it. What more could any feline ask for?

Jerri Brouillette would like to assure one and all that a new cat will be coming to NWSCF sometime this Summer. It's already been approved and is now just a matter of finding the right one.

Reprinted from *The Church at Prison Newsletter*, May, 1997

Paying Homage to the "Ramen Empire"

by J. Lee Mackenzie

I am currently a resident at the Chittenden Regional Correctional Facility. Built in the 1970s, the foundation of the facility has many cracks in it. As a result of these cracks (or as a result of their pure mining ingenuity), swarms of small brown ants have tunneled through the concrete and entered the cells of the facility all over the building. I have lived in all parts of the building during my time here and have found that these little brown ants have a vast empire of colonies that completely pervade the facility. They have total access to the whole building and come and go as they wish.

I have watched people engage in a futile struggle of wills with these tiny ants on many occasions as they invade the cells looking for the smallest scraps of food. The most common food source the small ants detect are the crumbs of "Ramen Noodles." As people break up these noodles, pieces inevitably drop unnoticed, but are hunted and retrieved by the ants as a source of essential nourishment.

At the vanguard of the troupe, the hunters of the colony, those who I call "sniffers," will trek out into the cell and roam bravely against the dangers of broom or foot, evading relocation or death, searching for crumbs. When they discover food they report back to the colony—at which point a large group of 20 or so ants will march out together like a team to bring the food home as quickly as possible. The way they navigate the floor reminds me of Bassett Hounds with their heads to the ground, sniffing and feeling their way around. But I've detected a problem with their strategy. Whenever they find sizable crumbs worth bringing home and send out a work force big enough to do the job, people get frustrated with the ants and sweep them up.

Bringing home the Ramen crumbs is a dangerous business, yet their entire empire relies on it. This is why I have come to call them "The Ramen Empire" or "The Ramens."

After watching the endless struggle between humans and Ramens, after watching countless people become annoyed and panic, and probably thousands of Ramens lose their lives, I have come up with a simple solution to the problem. But before I explain the simplicity of that solution, I must first tell another story.

While in another facility in Kentucky, I had an experience that changed my view of insects. In Kentucky inmates collected praying mantises, which were quite plentiful in that area. They would often keep them and arrange fights between them, which were matches to the death as one mantis would always win and eat the other. The fights were so popular people would bet commissary food items on them.

Most people would keep their mantises in boxes. However, we had one that lived free-range in the cell, wandering wherever it wished. This expanded freedom created a much better relationship with the mantis, who became a champion and never lost a fight. Mantises kept in boxes were typically harder for people to manage, more emotional and harder to control. They would fight keeper and opponent alike.

But not our mantis.

Ours would only fight other mantises, and because it always won people would have to pay us commissary. They didn't realize that the very food they were betting against us was our mantis' secret weapon. We were feeding it the commissary: bologna, macaroni, Ramen Noodles, almost anything. It was shocking how many different things it would eat!

Who knows whether our mantis was a girl or a boy, but we called it "him" and named *him* "Mikey" (after the old Kix commercial, "Give it to Mikey; he'll eat anything"). And Mikey did eat just about anything, even other bugs. Due to his enriched diet, Mikey grew a harder shell and tougher skin than any other mantises. In fact, Mikey had armor—which helped him to win all his fights.

Outside of the fights is where things began to get interesting. The more time we spent with Mikey, the more we began to learn about his character and ability to learn. First off, praying mantises, unlike many insects, have what appear to be visible pupils; they can turn their heads and make direct eye contact with you. We began to notice that when a group of us were talking, Mikey would look at whoever was speaking. I do not know if it was because of our words or gestures, but Mikey also learned to interact with us. When we offered Mikey food, he would come over.

When you asked Mikey if he wanted to be picked up, he would raise his arms like hooks, and you could scoop him up with a finger and put him on your shoulder. Once on your shoulder, if another person Mikey knew said, "Hey Mikey, come here," Mikey would fly over and land on the person's shoulder (or head). It was a little scary at first because a huge mantis makes a thundering, fan-like sound as it flies at your head, but we got used to it quickly as the act itself was amazing.

Soon Mikey was hanging out with us all the time, like "one of the boys." Mikey would watch TV with us, make eye contact with whoever was speaking, and became more like a friend. Our affinity grew so great that we eventually stopped fighting Mikey. In fact, we stopped fighting mantises altogether and spent more time trying to understand them. Mikey went on to teach us as much or more than we taught him—he made us look at all insects differently.

Unfortunately, Mikey was killed in 2004 when the facility was taken over in a prison riot. It was quite a bizarre way to end the interesting and memorable life of an unlikely and unforgettable character.

But Mikey will always be remembered.

Years later, before being shipped back to Chittenden from a facility in Newport, I watched a program on TV about insects and their ability to learn. The show investigated training wasps to find cadavers. They would teach them in a laboratory by putting the wasps in a container with a tiny hole in it and present them with the smell of decaying human flesh. When the wasp went to the smelling hole, it would be given a drop of sugar water. After repeating this process only three times a wasp would be completely trained and could sniff for human flesh as well as a dog.

The investigators would place three wasps together in a container with a sniffing hole and put it on the bottom of a device that looked like a metal detector to sweep the ground. There was a camera that focused on the wasps' movements and filtered it through a computer that would recognize when the wasps would swarm the "smelling hole" (which they only did when they sensed human remains). They were extremely effective and accurate, and this method introduced an excellent way to find dead bodies.

As I got back to Chittenden I observed the ongoing struggle between people and the Ramens. After a particularly rough week of casualties for the little crumb-hunters, I couldn't help but reflect on my experience with Mikey and the program about the "cadaver wasps." That was when I came up with my simple idea. I got my cellmate to stop sweeping them up and throwing them away, and we took a moment to take a closer look at them.

I watched the Ramens drag small crumbs long distances to a small hole, noticing how many it took to accomplish such an amazing feat. It occurred to me that they had been here doing this since long before I was even born in order to feed their "people." I thought to myself, *Do we really have to kill a hundred of these guys over a few crumbs?* There had to be a more reasonable way to conduct the dynamic of our relationship. Nobody wants the room they live in to be raided daily by ants, but the Ramens don't want to starve or die either.

Upon studying the Ramens, I found that they could smell very effectively and can feel around well, but long treks can be very dangerous because they can't see. Their eyes are nothing more than little sensors, only detecting light and dark. They can't discern visual shapes and patterns, but if you wave a hand blocking the light cast over them, the movement of the shadow scares them and they run.

Based on these observations, alongside what I learned from Mikey and the cadaver wasps, I devised a new strategy to deal with their daily invasions of our privacy. Instead of killing the Ramens, I would take three simple steps: reduce the distance they had to travel for crumbs; give them a small pile of crumbs daily; and only feed them at night after dark. To do this, each evening before bed, I put one decent pile of Ramen noodle crumbs in front of only one of their holes. (They had three holes in my cell. *Or was it their cell?*)

Within a few days the Ramens completely stopped using their other two holes. They stopped coming out during the day and only came out at night when I put crumbs in front of their hole. After placing the bait I watched at night as one ant would come out looking for food. When it detected the noodle crumbs, as expected, it reported the presence of food back to the ant colony. Then a huge army of ants would come out and swarm the one-inch area in front of their hole, bringing the food back through the hole to their hideout.

Since conducting this experiment my cell hasn't been raided by ants. They only come out at night and only target the pile of crumbs by their hole, leaving the rest of my cell untouched. Now we live in virtual harmony each and every day.

The only other time I see the Ramens is when I accidentally drop a crumb in front of their hole, which is rare. Even then, only a few come out as most have learned not to come out during daylight.

Another thing to be noted is that the small Ramen are not as wise or knowledgeable as the bigger ones, who seem to have grown and learned more, or who have more experience outside the hole. You can see the difference between the big, medium-sized, and tiny workers. The tiny ones sometimes hinder a food-retrieval project by pulling a piece of food in the wrong direction or by fumbling in their handling of the food. They also panic more and run aimlessly when scared. When frantic, they do not correct themselves well or find their way to the hole very quickly. The big, mature soldier ants and medium-sized workers are more accurate in bringing food in the right direction and more coordinated in maneuvering food items together. Although they still make a few mistakes in teamwork, they correct themselves much more easily.

I've found that the bigger Ramen are wiser and act more calmly under pressure. When they get scared, they don't become as blinded by fear. They may run in the wrong direction for a brief moment, but then correct themselves and run back in the direction of the hole. The bigger ones are better at navigation as their experience has given them better skills.

Aside from differences in age, experience and size, one thing is for sure: they all work very hard and seem quite content when doing so. Their amazing work ethic reminds me of the Seven Dwarfs on their way to the mine, singing: "Hi Ho, Hi Ho. It's off to work we go!"

Though some of my cohorts chalk it up to an in-born instinct, having observed the Ramen for some time, I think much of their devoted work ethic is learned from each other, through experience and interactions with their environment. They are highly social creatures, very fast learners, and constantly strive to maintain their livelihood.

In honoring the mutually beneficial arrangement we have developed, I've experimented with giving them crumbs of different foods. In so doing, I've discovered that Ramen noodles are a staple item, but mostly a food of convenience, and that they enjoy a wide variety of foods. As it turns out, just like me, one of their favorite foods is chocolate!

The question posed at the onset of my experiment was: "Do I have to kill hundreds of these little guys over crumbs?" The results of the experiment show that the answer is a resounding "No!" The Ramen learned to adapt to a situation which was better for me and my kind in a way that causes us no trouble. The experiment showed that a small effort can sometimes go a long way.

If I could teach the rest of the guys around here how to employ a simple trick that can drastically improve the dynamic of their relationship with the Ramen, many more ant lives would be saved. After all, the little fellas were here long before us, and will be here long after. Somehow, I think the other guys would be hard to teach. But as long as I'm in this cell, and in whatever cell I go to, the Ramen can experience a time of peace, and our arrangement will be honored.

With some questions answered and some lessons learned, I can't help but be left with a few final thoughts. In this complicated world we live in, one of our greatest goals should be to learn. What good is our conscious mind if not for that? And if insects can learn, with their limited understanding of reality and within their own peculiar mode of perception, then how different are we from them? Are they lower lifeforms? Or do they simply exist at a different wavelength of the same source of light and life?

While these questions are moreover to be pondered than answered, one thing I have found is that a vital step in bridging the gap between myself and other life forms, whatever wavelength or place in the world it comes from, is to give it a name. Naming other creatures makes it easier for us to see them as individuals with actual identities, whatever their form may be. And looking at the individual is how we learn about the whole. It teaches us to have greater empathy and deeper understanding in all our relationships.

With that said, as I have written at an appropriate length about the subjects on my mind, I will close with the thought that now perhaps more than a small handful of people will know that a praying mantis by the name of "Mikey" once lived, fought, learned, and died amongst men. But, most importantly, he taught and showed us a quality of character, not so much as would be expected from the world of bugs, but as if out of the Roman Colosseum, the story of a captured slave turned gladiator, who won the hearts of the people and went on to become a scholar and ambassador for the world of bugs.

Like Mikey, the ambassador mantis, the Ramen have shown how we are all interconnected in life...

The Book "Bible"

by Moses Cirrilo

As a teenager, I remember walking side by side with my mother to church every Sunday. At that age I had no intention to read the book "Bible" myself. Then, all of a sudden, I found myself in one of the most quiet places in the world, the Sahara Desert. Knowing that I would spend more than a year there, and having a Bible with me, I decided for my first time to read the Bible myself. Even though I did not understand all of the spiritual messages in the Bible, it is the only precious book I have ever read.

Coming to the U.S. and applying for political asylum, the idea that I would spend three years in jail was the farthest thing from my mind. But God knows what is ahead of me more than I do. And, once again, I found myself in a place where I would have more time to read His words, and so I did.

This book "Bible" contains the mind of God, the state of man, the way of Salvation, the doom of sinners and the happiness of believers. Its doctrines are holy, its precepts are binding, its histories are true, and its decisions are immutable.

It contains light to direct you, food to support you, and comfort to cheer you. It is the traveler's map, the pilgrim's staff, the pilot's compass, the soldier's sword, and the Christian's character. Here paradise is restored, heaven opened and the gates of hell disclosed. Christ is its grand object. Our goodness is its design. And the glory of God its end. It should fill the memory, rule the heart, and guide the feet.

Read it to be wise, believe it to be safe, and practice it to be holy. Read it slowly, frequently, and prayerfully. It is given to you in life, and will be opened in judgement, and remembered forever. It involves the highest responsibility and the greatest reward, but will condemn all who trifle with its sacred contents.

Read it and find out yourself.

God Bless You!
Moses Cirrilo
Franklin County Jail

Addendum: Moses Cirrilo is from the African country of Sudan where Arab Moslems have taken over the government and have been making war against Christian natives like Moses. Moses' wife and child were killed before he fled Sudan.

Moses was unable to obtain a passport and visa from Sudan and finally was able to come to the US using illegal papers. Upon arrival in New York he was incarcerated pending his request for political asylum.

After being denied twice in Federal court, he appealed to the US Immigration Board of Appeals. Finally, after more than three years of waiting in jail, he was granted asylum and the right to apply for US citizenship.

During his incarceration Moses was an active evangelist in jail and kept us busy ordering Foreign Language Bibles for other INS prisoners from all over the world.

Today Moses is a productive member of American society.

Close Custody Deliverance

by Rich Gardner

I was alone, confined in a close custody disciplinary unit, aka solitary confinement. At first the peace and solitude was good because it helped me seek and worship the Lord. I had repented of the error of my ways and was seeking Him more, wanting to be in fellowship with my Savior. Reading, studying, and worshipping consumed a good portion of my days.

As the days went on though, I found myself missing my Christian brothers in the Church. I was missing a lot of things, finding it harder to focus on God and not on my circumstances. Loneliness, self pity, and frustration set in, and I felt as if no one cared about me.

I was stressed out, even to the point of thinking about hurting myself, when Pastor Pete came to visit me. Seeing my emotional state and hearing my corresponding thoughts, he said, "We need to pray." Confessing my self-pity as sin, in Jesus' name we cast out the tormenting evil spirits and invited the Holy Spirit to take charge of my life once again.

The results were swift in coming. All the anxiety, depression, self-pity, and destructive thoughts left me. We talked further on positive matters before Pastor Pete departed. Now I was able to focus again on my fellowship with God and worshipping Him.

God delivered me from a downward spiral, the trap of Satan's evil spirits, and set my feet back on the Rock of my Salvation.

In God alone we find our strength. He will take care of the rest.

Thanks you Lord Jesus.

Praise your holy name.

Amen!

Kairos #11 – Testimony

by Glen Hall

I had a massive headache for a good five hours before I went to Kairos, which got worse when I arrived. After being there for an hour I decided it was not for me.

I sat around waiting for "my escape," wanting to leave without being noticed. Before I could get out we were all moved into the chapel. While sitting there I made a halfhearted prayer to God: if He would get rid of my headache, I would stay for the Kairos weekend. After about 15 minutes of sitting there with my temples pounding, I said to myself, "Yea right, so much for that!" Then the headache left, so I stayed the rest of that evening.

That night I was playing ping-pong with one of the guys when the thought entered my mind that I wouldn't go to Kairos for the next three days—within minutes my headache came back worse than before. I couldn't move fast or bend over to pick up the ball or my head would begin to throb. I didn't say anything to anyone, but I did say inwardly, "OK Lord, I'll go the next three days to Kairos." The headache again left within minutes. There were no bright lights, but it was my sign that God was telling me it was time to give my life over to Jesus Christ, which is what I did the next day.

Witnessing

by Bob Sawyer

I don't know about you, but I have often found witnessing to be a tricky business. It isn't so much what to say but when to say it that often befuddles me. There's an old maxim, "timing is everything." Well, to the Spiritual man, the Lord is everything, but He would often have us pay more attention to timing with our words.

Now, there are various kinds of witnessing, but timing comes into play with all of them. We, of course, witness to non-believers about the basic Gospel message. We also witness to brothers and sisters in the Lord when we have a message to share. And we bear witness to ourselves by the way we act and react, especially in a public setting. This third version is vitally important in a place like prison where we live in an enclosed society that encounters itself constantly.

So, what is our approach? Well, let's take a look at Scripture for direction.

First, we must be prayerful ... no surprise there. When the apostles were unable to expel demons from a dumb boy, Jesus cautioned them about the need for prayer (*Mark 9:28-29*). In other words, action in the Lord had to be timed to follow a period of preparation.

Then there are situations (and this happens in prison all the time) where you're standing in line and the person in front of you issues a Scriptural or theological challenge. It may be something like an Old Testament dietary law that relates to that day's lunch or some other such issue. Before engaging your mouth, think about what Paul wrote to Timothy about arguing (*2 Timothy 2:23-26*). Pray about the timing of your intended remarks and decide whether the setting is appropriate for a serious dialogue as opposed to a dumb shouting match.

Sometimes you want to share a personal insight you think will be helpful, but the other person doesn't respond. This happens a lot in our Bible studies where discussions about theology can become argumentative. Jesus reminded his disciples that not everyone has the ears to hear (*Matthew 11:13-15*) and often it is (you guessed it) timing that makes the difference. A private dialogue might do the trick when someone is embarrassed in a public setting. Remember, Stephen told the crowd that wanted to kill him that he could see Jesus, and their response was to cover their ears and stone him (*Acts 7:57*).

Some people just won't listen when you want them to.

As for bearing witness to ourselves, being incarcerated offers many opportunities, both bad and good. Here's some advice, don't try to minister to someone after receiving a disciplinary report—you may encounter deaf ears. You also may find that your transgression leads another to stray, and that's not good at all (*Romans 14:20 -21*). The Bible doesn't demand perfection, but it does tell us to be faithful to the Lord if we expect to see fruit in our ministries ... and that's especially true of witnessing.

Again, your timing can be critical.

One final point, don't try to influence unbelievers by feeding into their weaknesses and misconceptions. I saw a recent example of this when efforts were being made to proclaim the veracity of Scripture to an educated person who believed in evolution. A discussion ensued about the literal meaning of certain words in the creation story. The nonbeliever was quite thrilled to hear that the Biblical descriptions may not be as literal as we think. Though this may, indeed, be true, because it fit into this person's preconceptions about God using evolution to create the world, I was concerned that the witnessing effort missed the mark. I recognize the fascination in studying the nuances of such topics, but I suggest the timing was off because it diverted this individual away from accepting the Bible as God's literal word.

If the creation story can be picked apart in a scholarly way, then what other Scriptures should we go after? We're much better off teaching newcomers to embrace the Bible literally and to let the indulgences of scholarship come later, as the Holy Spirit guides us.

You see, it's all in the timing.

Renewal of Love after 34 Years

" a three-fold cord is not easily broken."
Eccl. 4:12

by Ramon Valentin

On Sunday night, the 23rd of January, I was honored by a special ceremony taking place in the church. Sister Agnes and Pastor Pete honored us by renewing their marriage vows after 34 years of marriage in a ceremony conducted by Pastor Steve Clark. Upon hearing and seeing them exchange their covenant vows, I was overwhelmed by varied emotions, but more importantly I was touched by the power of the Holy Spirit. I felt as though we were in the presence of God Almighty, standing in His throne-room.

While listening to their vows of commitment and seeing the face of Sister Agnes radiate with joy and excitement, I asked the Lord to allow me the opportunity to renew these vows of commitment with my wife when He delivers me back to society. At that moment, I began to see the ceremony in a different light. I saw my Lord and Savior Jesus Christ saying to me:

> I, the Lord of heaven and earth, vow my blood covenant, which was poured out on Calvary, that I will be your protector, your healer. I will provide for you like no one else can. I will be with you in your lowest moments and I will rejoice with you when you are most happy. Understand too, I will never give up on you, I will be with you forever, for my love for you is endless.

Seeing Pastor Pete and Sister Agnes embrace and kiss each other, I was overwhelmed with emotion and tears. Yes, Jesus loves me, for no other man could have ever done what He did for me, giving me a new life filled with hope.

Thank you Pastor Pete and Sister Agnes for sharing such an intimate moment with a bunch of men, many who may have been witnessing and understanding for the very first time what the marriage ceremony is really all about. There were few dry eyes during this special moment, but above all, the glory of God was felt in a very special way.

Restitution, Inc.

by Betsy Wolfenden

Although I entered law school in the Fall of 1996 with the goal of becoming a tax attorney, I was drawn to a meeting of a legal organization called The Death Penalty Project. At the meeting I learned that defense attorneys working on capital cases needed law student volunteers to help out with their defendants' appeals. Because of family responsibilities, I was forced to limit my involvement to becoming a pen-pal to someone who had been sentenced to death. After reading a number of introductory letters from death row inmates seeking pen-pals, I made my choice. The inmate's name was Michael Fullwood.

Michael and I wrote to each other for a year, and I began visiting him during my second year of law school. I knew from our letters and conversations that Michael was an accomplished artist and on one visit I asked him what he would like to do with his artwork. Michael paused, then said, "I want to make restitution." Michael's response surprised me. Michael had killed his daughter's mother when his daughter, named Michelle, was just an infant, and I was not sure how someone could make restitution for such a horrible crime.

On my next visit to the prison, I proposed to Michael the idea of starting a college fund for Michelle. Michael had seen an ad in an art magazine for a company that made note cards from original paintings and drawings, so we decided to sell cards made from his artwork and use the proceeds to fund Michelle's college account. It took us another six months to work out all the details, but by the fall of my third year of law school we had 1,000 boxes of beautiful note cards ready to sell and a college fund set up at the bank.

I sent one of the first boxes of cards to Michelle's grandmother who was raising Michelle. She shared them with Michelle who was thrilled to learn that not only did her dad love her, he wanted to help her attend college. For the first time in fifteen years, Michael and Michelle began communicating.

In 1998, Michael and I co-founded the nonprofit Restitution Incorporated, with the goal of promoting healing between offenders and victims. Our first project is The National Death Row Inmate Restitution Art Show, scheduled to open in early 2000. We are assembling artwork from death row inmates around the country and will be displaying their work on our website. Commemorative prints of some of the original work will be available, and the proceeds from donations will go to either surviving victims or charitable organizations.

In addition to the art show, we have an "Apologies" section on our website for inmates who would like to apologize to their victims. Many inmates are extremely remorseful and we would like those inmates to have a place to share their spiritual and emotional growth. We have also started to work directly with more victims. One inmate who committed murder requested that I ask his victim's mother if she would accept a letter of apology from him. I was able to find her and she agreed to receive his letter. She told me that she did not hate her son's killer. In addition, members of a rape survivor's group recently visited our site to read the words written by an inmate who is serving two life sentences for kidnapping and rape. The women told us they found his testimony healing.

I graduated from law school in July of 1999. Somewhere in the middle of my studies I realized the sole purpose of living is to serve God. In my case, that means helping those whose lives have been affected by violent crime. Making a whole bunch of money as a tax attorney pales by comparison.

Odds and Ends

by Bob Sawyer

It has been a while since I contributed to this newsletter. Last November, I was transferred to Virginia and found it difficult to write. On the 6th of April, I was brought back to Vermont for a court hearing, but was placed in the Newport facility instead of St. Albans, where I had been for seven years. I have been here in Newport for a month and decided it was a good time to say a few things to you folks out there.

My court business is finished and I have yet to be told whether or not to expect a return to the Old Dominion (as the natives call it). But, whether I stay in Vermont or head South again, there is something you should know. The spiritual situation in both facilities is not healthy, from a Christian perspective, and much prayer is needed. The specifics for both locations are different but the end result is the same.

The problem in Virginia is that all Christian activities are inmate-run, under the general direction of the facility Chaplain. This has led, in recent months, to an inconsistent leadership. Strong brothers from places like Michigan recently left to go home and, when I left, there seemed to be a lack of spiritual guidance. Add to this the fact that there is competition for space among various religious groups, Christian and non-Christian, and you have a scenario wherein the Christians from Vermont must be very assertive and this is not always easy,
especially for younger brothers who lack experience. Attempts have been made to have prayer sessions in the yard and Bible studies in the unit day rooms, but many of the men feel self-conscious or even intimidated about

public displays. Again, this problem can be especially acute for our newer brothers.

Another issue in Virginia is a cultural difference in the way services are run. There is much emphasis placed on emotion and physical displays, such as jumping up and down and shouting responses to whoever is speaking. Now, please do not misunderstand. There is definitely a place for Godly emotion in worship, but I have observed a discomfort with some of the Vermont brothers and have learned that some are reluctant to attend services because of this cultural difference.

What I am asking for is prayer from all of you about this as well as written support. The men down there need to hear from you. They need to know that, even though they are hundreds of miles away, the Lord is with them and you are with them in your hearts and prayers.

The situation in Newport needs evangelism and commitment. There are some strong brothers in the faith, but there needs to be more activities and more effort placed on personal outreach. It saddens me to report that we only get 6 to 8 men out to a Bible study. Since there are more than 300 here, I have to believe that many Christians need to be made aware of the need for fellowship and how much we want to know them. The men at Northwest in St. Albans have a wonderful Christian environment. Praise for the Saviour should be a part of everyone's prayer life who is there, along with prayer for their brothers in Newport and Virginia.

I want to share something that came from my friend, Betty Powell, in Australia. Betty recently sent me two testimonies and I have her permission to share them with you.

#1: "On Sunday night after church, we were around the table and all of a sudden there came a mighty rushing wind and rain pouring on the roof. My friends started exclaiming, 'It's raining.' I said, 'No way! There's not a cloud in the sky.'

With that I went out into the back yard. The moon was shining bright, the stars were twinkling, and the sky was clear. There had definitely been a mighty move of the Holy Spirit over my house."

#2: "For the last 10 to 12 weeks, the ceiling in my room has been lit up with stars shining bright, and oh, such a glory cloud. Also, at times, there has been such clarity of swift bright flashes across the room and in the lounge and dining room. There is only love, joy, and peace flowing. Through it all, sometimes I feel I've just walked into an angel and such laughter flows. It's definitely a heavenly visitation and, oh, how all the bodily aches and pains are lifted to allow me a good night's sleep."

I don't know about you but I would like to visit Betty's house sometime.

Being a Father in Jail

by Bob Sawyer

Incarceration is tough on fathers. In fact, being kept from my children is the single most difficult part of imprisonment for me. After two years, missing the companionship of my sons brings about the deepest, most difficult emotions and the most profound regrets.

I have three sons, all young teenagers, who are growing up without my physical presence in their daily lives. They live two hundred miles from NWSCF—and I only see them three times a year, for six-hour visits on the three Family Days provided by the facility—yet the Lord has shown me things about this situation which I would like to share.

The quality of a relationship is what counts, and the spiritual quality of fatherhood, even from prison, is the key to success. I pray for the boys every day, and I keep them in my heart in a way that I never did before incarceration. Part of this is having the time to focus on them and their needs. Part of it is the acceptance of their need for me in their lives, even at a distance. And, part of it (the biggest part) is my commitment to Jesus, which brings blessings upon their lives as well as my own.

I write them each and every week. Sometimes, the letters are short, sometimes they are lengthy. It might be just a quick "hello" or it might be a lengthy discourse on a subject like "keeping up their studies." The point is that the letters come every week, one to each of them. I know they read them and I know they're glad to receive them. If they decide to respond or make any comment about what I've written, that's frosting on the spiritual cake.

Of course, I call them ... but not as often as I would like. Phone calls are expensive and I have no income. Still, the Lord sees to it that I talk to them a couple of times a month.

When visits do occur, I maintain a positive and upbeat demeanor. They want to know that I am OK—this is really important to them. They ask me questions about what I do, how I'm treated, and whether I'm safe. I have been amazed at just how much reassurance they need about my well-being. I remind them that the Lord is looking after all of us, and that gives them a sense of wholeness and peace. They can see that I am still a viable human being and still very much their dad.

One reaction that delighted me came from my middle son, who suggested during the last Family Day that I was "more of a father now than before." That, I knew, was God's work. No doubt about it. After two years and two hundred miles, he saw me *as more of a Dad, not less*. I believe the Lord was honoring the prayer time and heart condition I had devoted to them and placed that observation on my son's tongue.

It is also true that my commitment to faith has a spiritual impact on them. They do not even realize how much they are being effected spiritually. They did tell me that they are Christians and I was pleased to hear that. They have their own work to do as they mature, and God will reveal His will to them in His time.

Meanwhile, I know that I must continue to press on for them and with them, despite the circumstances that keep me in here. It's not a chore; it's a blessing.

It's fatherhood. And it can be practiced in jail. Take it from one who knows.

Testimony of Pastor Fred Little

A series of hasty decisions made in response to unexpected circumstances yielded the worst possible outcome—death. Bearing the responsibility for ending a person's life prematurely and realizing I had broken the hearts of all the people connected to that life, including my own, had driven me to a point of utter despair.

Plagued by guilt, depression, and suicidal thoughts, I merely existed during the first few months of incarceration. Sleeping and watching TV provided a temporary escape from the ever-present reality that my deeds had given rise to. But the torment of my soul seemed inescapable. I felt caught between the rock and the proverbial hard place. Part of me wanted to die to end the pain, but another part of me didn't want to cause my loved ones any additional heartache.

Desperate for relief and at my wits end, I decided to seek out the prison pastor so that I could unload my burden on him. I had previously observed this man, whom others referred to as "Pastor Pete," meeting regularly with men during the week. Having heard many good things about him, I figured I had nothing to lose and made an appointment to meet with him.

Pastor Pete greeted me with a welcoming smile and a firm handshake on the day of our initial meeting and invited me to have a seat so that we could get acquainted. After a brief conversation about our individual life histories, he asked me what it was that he could do for me specifically. I responded by telling him I just needed someone to talk to who would guarantee to maintain confidentiality in our conversation—which he willingly agreed to do.

Pastor Pete listened to me empathetically on that providential day as I expressed feelings that had long been held captive. What a relief it was to finally have someone listen to me without questioning or making a judgment about what I was saying. We concluded our time together with a prayer and a mutual agreement to meet again the following week. I left his company that day greatly relieved and looking forward to our next appointment.

Our second appointment began with a brief prayer followed by a serious question about destiny. "Fred, where would your soul/spirit go if you were to die tonight," Pastor Pete asked. I didn't really know what to say, but responded by telling him that I hoped that I would go to heaven when I die. "Don't you want to be sure about that?" he continued. My answer was, "Well yes, but how can I be sure?" He went on to explain that I first had to pray and admit I was a sinner—that I had broken at least one of the 10 commandments and consequently fallen short of meeting God's standard for living.

The penalty for sin, Pastor Pete explained, is death—separation from God forever in the place of eternal torment called Hell. He then told me the good news: that Jesus Christ laid down His life for me as payment for my sins and was raised from the dead to justify me in God's sight. He went on to say if I believed that truth and confessed it openly I would be guaranteed a home in heaven upon my death. Well, that was an offer that was too good to refuse, because I knew that I had broken almost all of the commandments and did not want to suffer the consequence of Hell. So I allowed Pastor Pete to lead me in a simple prayer of repentance, and from that day forward in June, 1995 my life has not been the same.

I have been a regular member of the Church at Northwest since the time of my conversion, and had the privilege of serving the Body of Christ in various ways over the years: setting up the visiting room for the worship service; taking attendance; facilitating a Christian literature and music library; operating the sound system; teaching Bible studies and college level classes; counseling other men; and eventually ministering in a pastoral capacity. I preach at least twice a month and have the responsibility of conducting the monthly communion service. I have also been involved in memorial services for those who have lost loved ones while in prison. Recently, I had the opportunity and privilege to officiate my first marriage ceremony.

Every one of the volunteer staff who I have come to know through the ministry of the Church at Prison have looked beyond the ugliness of my sinful past and have embraced me as the new creation that God declares me to be in His everlasting word. They have openly demonstrated that they are

Christ's disciples through their action of loving and discipling someone like me—one considered least in the eyes of the world. I could not have survived this time in prison without God's presence expressed through those faithful folks who serve Him in the prison ministry, and I will forever be indebted to God for sending them to walk with me throughout my incarcerated state. Without them, as David wrote, I would have lost heart ... (*Ps. 27:13*).

Through the gospel ministry of the Church at Prison and the friendships that I am privileged to share with the volunteers and members therein, God saved my life and afforded me the preparatory training to do what He has called me to do. He has redeemed this time of incarceration for His purposes by allowing me to gain necessary experience inside the prison that will benefit me on the outside—for which I am truly grateful.

In closing, I leave you with Paul's words which summarize my testimony and reflect how I feel about the unmerited grace that God has bestowed upon my life.

> I thank Christ Jesus our Lord, who has given me strength, that he considered me faithful, appointing me to his service. Even though I was once a blasphemer and a persecutor and a violent man, I was shown mercy because I acted in ignorance and unbelief. The grace of our Lord was poured out on me abundantly, along with the faith and love that are in Christ Jesus. Here is a trustworthy saying that deserves full acceptance: Christ Jesus came into the world to save sinners—of whom I am the worst. But for that very reason I was shown mercy so that in me, the worst of sinners, Christ Jesus might display his unlimited patience as an example for those who would believe on him and receive eternal life. Now to the King eternal, immortal, invisible, the only God, be honor and glory for ever and ever. Amen (*1 Tim 1:12-17*).

Rafael's Story
"Historia de la Vida en el Mar"

by Rafael Mercedes Senereno

Originally from The Dominican Republic, Rafael Mercedes Senereno is a Spanish speaking inmate at The Franklin County Jail in St. Albans. He has been incarcerated there for several months awaiting disposition by Federal Court. Rafael has been growing in faith as a result of his incarceration as times of distress bring many people closer to God. During Sunday Church service at the jail, Rafael always adds his own message of encouragement to Hispanics after the preaching message.

At 12:00 midnight, February 22, 1995, alongside one hundred and twenty five comrades, I set out in a crowded boat for Puerto Rico in search of a better life. At noon the next day, we were entering The Canal de la Mena when one of the motors seized. We tried to fix it, but it was in vain. The rush of the waves increased and the passengers began falling faint, vomiting and weeping. Amidst the turmoil, a group of Haitian Christians began to read the Bible, pray, sing Christian Hymns, and claim the name of the Lord our Savior. The waves began to calm and, little by little, the sea became serene. We continued on our journey with only one motor and arrived in Puerto Rico safely.

It was at this time that I began to believe in God. Before this, I was an unbeliever, because I viewed the Word of God as a weapon of the wealthy against the poor. Today I believe in God as the almighty and only Savior of the World.

Now when He got into a boat, His disciples followed Him. Suddenly a great storm arose on the sea so that the boat was covered with the waves. But He was asleep. Then His disciples came to Him and awoke Him, saying, "Lord, save us! We are perishing." But He said to them, "Why are you fearful, O you of little faith?" Then He arose and rebuked the winds and the sea. And there was a great calm. And the men marveled, saying, "Who can this be, that even the winds and the sea obey Him?" (*Matthew 8:23-27*).

Choices
by Fernand Forcier

It came and it went, this moment in time,
For all to see, only a few to find.
Before their eyes the word expressed,
Too good to believe, they put Him to the test.

With love and compassion He responded to each one,
To the very end, when he said, "Now it is done."
As we stand on the threshold of life's eternity,
With joy in each heart, with friends and family.

How long we have waited, how many times we've been told
That the streets of that city are paved with purest gold.
Now that day approaches for those who are blessed,
Who have walked that last mile and have passed the test.

With each fleeting moment an opportunity is lost,
I ask you my friend, did you ever count the cost,
Of living your life throughout eternity,
Separated from the one who dies for you and me.

This life presents many choices, and at the very best,
If we choose to follow JESUS, He will surely give you rest
From life's oft constant struggles and disappointment's bitter pain,
If we live our life for Him, He will send the latter rain.

So my friend this poem is almost over,
I've said all that I can.

The choice now rests on you, won't you take Him,
The Great "I AM."

VI.

MEMORIALS, FUNERALS & REMEMBRANCES

Marian

by Fred Little

On March 18, 2006 relatives and friends gathered at Essex Alliance Church in Essex to celebrate the life and to mourn the death of Marian Fay, who died at age 92. Marian traveled to NWSCF in St. Albans every week. In later years even blindness did not stop her from ministering to the men at NWSCF. The picture on the left is the celebration of her 90th birthday at NWSCF. Her dear friend Bettie Clark is helping her cut the cake.

I have heard it said that a picture is worth a thousand words. So, when Pastor Pete asked me to write a brief article about how the late Marian Fay had touched my life, I decided to include a picture that I feel illustrates the kind of friendship that I shared with Marian.

As you can see (on the next page), the picture is that of a mother lovingly embracing her infant son. The viewer is left to imagine what is going on within the soul of each one as they look into each other's eyes. Perhaps the mother is silently thanking God for the blessing of this precious child—seeing in her mind's eye the great man that he will one day become. While, at the same time, the little one is marveling within himself about how good he feels when ever this lady picks him up. What ever the case may be, the unconditional and relational love shared between a mother and a son is clearly seen in the photo—the kind of love that I was blessed to share with Marian Fay.

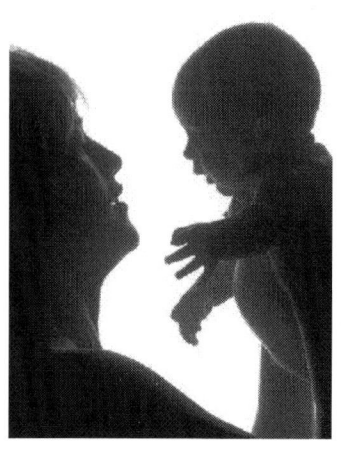

From the day that we first met, Marian Fay embraced me and loved me as if I was her natural son. She visited me regularly and corresponded with me often. She enthusiastically taught me truth from God's Word and about life. She prayed for me faithfully, encouraged me compassionately, and even rebuked me sternly whenever I needed it. Marian was a constant source of encouragement to me and always made me feel like a person of worth whose friendship she valued greatly. Her steadfast presence and unconditional love were instrumental in helping me through the last decade of my incarcerated life, and I will forever be grateful to God for sending His love to me through the life of such a virtuous and Spirit-filled lady.

PS: It is written in the book of Proverbs that a person is known by what others say of them (*Prov.27:21*). And Jesus said that His disciples would be known by their love for one another (*John 13:35*). As you reflect on what I have written here, you will realize that Marian Fay was a disciple of Jesus Christ who understood that love is expressed through action—even unto those considered least among us. Our challenge is to live and love as Marian Fay did, by inviting Jesus Christ to be the Lord of our lives, and by expressing our love for Him by keeping His Word.

Letter from an Offender's Wife

4.15.98

To Whom It May Concern:

My life will never be the same because of the outreach of The Church at Prison and Peter and Agnes Fiske. Although I have never served any time behind bars, I am very much a product of prison ministry.

    At the time my husband of eleven years was incarcerated, we had both been very active in our home church. His arrest and subsequent incarceration caused discomfort on both sides, leaving me feeling rejected and without the church family that I had learned to love.

    Those first few months of separation were some of the most difficult times I have ever lived through. I don't remember many details, just feeling numb and crying a lot. I was close to suicide—or so I thought. Then my husband was transferred to Northwest and began attending services there. When we talked he would share that was being taught at Bible study and how much the support of Pete and Agnes meant to him. I asked him if he thought they might be willing to be of support to me as well. Bruce asked and the answer came back that I would have to contact them personally—something I did not expect to have to do; in fact, I didn't think I could.

    It took a couple of weeks to work up the courage to call—after all, I was strong and could do anything alone. During the call I made an appointment to meet the Fiskes at their home. That appointment turned out to be dinner shared with their family and a visiting Christian musician on his way to the facility for a concert. Agnes gently guided me through my feelings of rejection, and eventually back to a one-on-one relationship with Christ. She also introduced me, indirectly, to another inmate's wife, who has become a good friend and Christian role model for me.

In September of this year I was diagnosed with a well advanced malignant tumor in my right lung. While I was in the hospital Pete and Agnes came and prayed with me and have remained in touch over the six months since, as I have struggled with chemotherapy. Never have I felt alone, for I have had my personal relationship with Christ to lean on. I now have a "church family" where I am loved and accepted. These beautiful people are constantly praying for me.

My husband was furloughed just before Christmas and has been welcomed into this church, where Christian volunteers who have been trained by The Church at Prison and Department of Corrections are working to re-integrate him into the community.

Thank you Pete and Agnes for being such willing servants, only God knows how many lives your ministry has changed. May God bless you and keep you.

Emma C. Duncan

Emma Duncan

Reprinted from May-June Newsletter

On June 15, 1998, Emma Duncan, beloved wife of Bruce Duncan, died at Dartmouth-Hitchcock Medical Center in Hanover, New Hampshire following a long battle with cancer.

We were able to say goodbye to our friend Emma, Saturday evening June 13. We visited with her relatives, prayed and sang hymns in the hospital room. God's peace and love was present.

The funeral was at the Lebanon Assembly of God Church.

Please pray for Bruce!

Bill Verrinder – Obituary

On Sunday, January 17, Bill Verrinder died at North West State Correctional facility in St. Albans, Vermont. Bill was born April 9, 1950. He was oldest of eleven children. After the death of his father, Bill helped his mother with the care of the family. He became like a father to his younger brothers and sisters.

At the age of 17, Bill joined the Marines and went to Vietnam, where he was a member of Bravo 19 Company, known as "The Walking Dead." Bill received decorations honoring his courage. He was involved in the famous Hamburger Hill Battle.

Bill went on to raise a family of his own and has two daughters and two sons that are described as "good kids" by Bill's brother Jim.

On Friday evening, January 22, the Church at Northwest held a Memorial Service for Bill where his fellow inmates were able to pay their respects to Bill and share their memories of him. The sharing time lasted about one hour. Consistently we heard that Bill was a good friend, helpful to new inmates, and developing his relationship with Jesus Christ. Two of Bill's poems were read by fellow inmates, Richard Kidson and Butch Bouchard.

Bill Verrinder Memorial

by Richard Kidson

Every human being, I believe, is a mystery to his or her fellow humans. In friendship, though, we try to at least reach out beyond those inevitable barriers. What could you ever really know about me, or I about any of you? What could we ever really know about William Verrinder. Probably what is most important about the shape of the soul is revealed in poetry... even inadvertently.

> Poetry is the voice
> of what has no voice,
> to tell the difference
> between sand and dirt,
> life and death,
> God and...
> love and...
> this other thing.

Poetry has long been the most popular form of literature in Vietnam, where poets are revered and highly respected. In Victnam, Bill Verrinder found this voice...as he stood between life and death. Bill was a student for a while in my writing class, until post-conviction relief issues began to consume his time. He asked me, though, if I would meet with him periodically, in private, to look at his poetry. In his always respectful way, he would approach me and say, "'Tuyan Quang' ('My Teacher'), would you look at this poem for me?"

Bill wrote a poem called 'An Uncovering.' Let me read it first, and then I will speak to it:

> An Uncovering
> (apokalypsis)
>
> Westward, over Phanom Dong Rak Mountains afar,
> far off I saw a Bright Star,
> hibiscus bloomed in her white hand.
> Rainbow robes
> trailing a broad sash,
> floating she brushes the heavenly stars
> and invites me to mount a cloud terrace
> to meet with God.
> Ravished, mad, I go with her, thinking
> I will talk to this God.
> There, I look down on Mekong River,
> a vast sea of barbarian soldiers marching,
> fresh blood spattered on the grasses of the wild,
> wolves, with men's hats on their heads;
> and then I look again to the rubble,
> to an old man of Phnom Penh.
> He was clothed in a robe which reached to His feet,
> His head and His hair were white like snow
> and His eyes were like a flame of fire.
> His voice was like the sound of many waters
> and his face was like the sun shining in its strength.
> A sign hung on his bombed-out shack,
>
> "Bring your guns here
> and I'll give you a plow."
>
> (Rev. 1:13-16; Isa. 2:4)
>
> by William Verrinder

In Western poetry, dreams of ascending are quite common because they refer to the vertical structure of the Western religious world—in contrast to the Eastern religions, where one is on a horizontal plane with God. In this poem, Bill has had a vision of a flight upward, following a goddess-like angel in a multi-colored robe set in contrast to a sudden sight of the earth below, the poor earth of misfortune after an invasion ... whereupon he has a realization as to who has the power to bring all war to an end.

Below the title of the poem, in parentheses, is the Greek word apokalypsis, which literally means 'to uncover' or 'to disclose' and is used most often regarding spiritual matters; thus we have the Biblical book called Revelation. To write this poem, Bill had to be familiar with the book of Revelation, and the prophetic Bible book of Isaiah. While Bill and I never had a spiritual conversation or a conversation about Jesus, I am convinced that probably what is most important about the shape of the soul is often revealed in poetry... even inadvertently.

James Hemingway – Obituary

by Sharon Andis

James "Jimmy" Hemingway died unexpectedly on March 8 at Greensville Correctional Center in Jarratt, Virginia.

He was born July 8, 1957 in St. Albans to the late Arthur and Frances Hemingway. He is survived by four brothers (George, Robert, Arthur, and Donald) and three sisters (Betty Beaty, Phyllis Camely, and Marilyn Perreault). His sister Janice died in 1998.

Jimmy's funeral was held at Elmwood-Muenier Funeral Home in Burlington on March 16. The service, conducted by Pastor Pete Fiske, was well attended by family and friends. On March 23 there was a memorial service held at NWSCF at the request of inmates that knew Jimmy.

During the Eulogy in Burlington, I shared the joys of meeting Jimmy and adopting his son Christopher. Here is what I said:

"My name is Sharon and I am the proud adoptive mom of Jim's son, Christopher. I think that if Jim were here tonight with all of these fresh flowers, he'd be handing them out to each of you. Jim had such a giving heart. He'd be saying, 'Which color do you like best? Red? Here, have this red one, and this one, here, take ALL of the red ones.' And then he'd turn to another person, asking, 'Which ones do you like best?' And you'd all be going home tonight with an armful of flowers.

"My son is the spittin' image of Jim. With the neatest personality of any child I've ever known, he carries on Jim's spirit. Christopher laid a Hot Wheels car on Jim's casket tonight because he shares Jim's love for cars and trucks. Jim had this dream of owning and driving a car one day ... and I want to tell you tonight that dream is going to be fulfilled ... in my son, Jim's son.

"Jim's path crossed mine a little over three years ago in a stiff conference room at the local hospital. He entered carrying a small bundle of baby boy swaddled in a blanket ... and I couldn't take my eyes off the wee lad in his arms. Jim was the proud Daddy that day and he brought tiny Christopher around to my side of the conference table and held him up in order to give me a better look. I was surprised when Jim asked if I would like to hold his son and was thrilled as he placed Christopher into my arms ... for I was eager to become this little boy's foster mom. Jim said, 'If you're going to be helping us take care of him, you may as well get acquainted,' and I was caught off guard by Jim's generosity. He allowed me to hold him past my first polite offer to return him ... even past my second offer ... all the way until the end of the awkward meeting, during which the social worker explained my helping role to Jim and his wife, Lori.

"From our first meeting, my heart hoped that this child would be my son while my mind tried unsuccessfully to warn me that this might not happen. But hearts have a way of winning.

"Jim acted as friend and mediator during our many visits over the weeks and months that followed. I was his son's foster mother, and yet Jim was kind and gracious towards me during our times together—which is remarkable!

"Jim often shared how much he had anticipated Christopher's arrival as his face shone with pride ... how he had chosen the child's name himself ... Christopher Allen Hemingway ... how much he had wanted a little boy, and how long he had waited for the joys of fatherhood.

"We met at that little church across the street (from the funeral home) one Sunday morning so that Jim and Lori could bring their son to the pastor for his dedication. Dress-up clothes, smiling faces, pride, joy, and purpose made their impressions upon the tiny church crowd during the solemn occasion that day.

"How honored I was when a few months later Jim stood in a courtroom to tell the judge that he wouldn't be able to take care of his son (after his arrest) and that he wanted the judge to let me be his mom. Later Jim said to me privately, "I can't take care of him now, so I want you to ... because I know you'll do a good job."

"Christopher became our 'Andy' and what a JOY he is! Although Jim and I have exchanged many letters and pictures during the past two years, the most memorable day was the day Andy (Christopher) and I visited Jim after he was incarcerated ... before Jim was transferred out-of-state and later out-of-town. We sat on the floor that day in awkward surroundings and zoomed trucks around on the floor ... simply for the response which would spread over Jim's son's, my son's, face. But I want to tell you tonight that the look on Andy's face that day paled in comparison to the look on Jim's face during the entire visit. Jim beamed with pride and joy, spoke often of his gratitude and thankfulness for our visit, our contact, my parenting of his son.

"I have always cherished the photos I took that day ... even more so today. They have become a very special page in Andy's baby album, and although I've been encouraged by some to remove that page from the album, to erase the memories, I will not do it. I stand firm in my belief that page of photos is to remain there because Jim is a part of my son's life and always will be. I want those of you who are Andy's relatives to have contact with him if you want. You, too, are part of his life.

"I feel sorry for you all because you will get up and leave here tonight with empty arms, grieving. And, I share in your grief. But, tonight, I get the privilege of leaving here with my son.

"I will miss Jim. Truly, I will.

"A piece of Jim lives on, though, and lights up my life. Jim's Christopher is now 3 ½ years old and my heart no longer wrestles with my mind over whether or not he will be my son. His adoption has been finalized, but, more importantly, he is etched upon my heart indelibly, and I upon his.

"Thank you, Jim, for your kindnesses, your words, and for the gift of your son. Thank you for your friendship. I am honored to be your friend and I miss you already."

With great love,
Sharon.

Remembering Jimmy

by Fred Little

I became acquainted with Jimmy while attending one of the weekly Bible studies here at NWSCF. He acted nervously shy at first, but once he got to know the group he became comfortable among us. Jimmy was always eager to display a picture of his young son for everyone to view and would always glow with prideful adoration while he told us about him. It was obvious to me that Jimmy loved his son very much. During one of the first few Bible studies that Jimmy attended, he happened to notice that I had a purple highlighter I used to mark my Bible. Following the study he approached me and excitedly said he wanted to give me something that he thought I would like. Not quite knowing how to react, I thanked him for his gesture and to be quite honest, forgot about it until the following week's class. It was then that Jimmy reminded me of the prior week's discussion.

Before the class started, Jimmy hurriedly approached me, barely able to contain his excitement, and asked, "Do you want to know what it is that I have for you?" I responded by saying, "Sure Jimmy, what have you got?" Quickly, he reached into his pocket and pulled out a used purple pen. Handing it to me with childlike enthusiasm he said, "I thought you'd like this because it matches your purple marker. I want you to have it." I accepted the pen and thanked him for his kindness, then proceeded to show it off to the rest of the group as a measure to build up Jimmy's spirits. You see, Jimmy was mentally disabled. I would say that he had the intellectual ability of an eight or ten year old child. Therefore, he needed much guidance, as would any person with this level of maturity—especially within the prison system, where people can be insensitive and sometimes abusive toward the mentally handicapped.

The Church at Northwest provided counseling for Jimmy that initially resulted in his becoming born again in the Spirit. Only the Lord knows whether or not Jimmy fully understood what that commitment meant. Jimmy also received counsel from the Church regarding his legal case. This resulted in his accepting responsibility for his actions, which led him to plead guilty to the crime that he had been charged with. Surely, this was a demonstration of repentance. The word of God says; "He who conceals his transgressions will not prosper, but he who confesses and forsakes them will find compassion" (*Proverbs 28:13*).

I still have that purple pen. It serves as a reminder of the cheerful spirit and boyish disposition that resided within the heart of the man known as Jimmy.

Jesus said: "Let the little children come to me, and do not hinder them, for the kingdom of God belongs to such as these. I tell you the truth, anyone who will not receive the kingdom of God like a little child will never enter it" (*Luke 18:16-17*).

Pastor's note: We have devoted substantial space in this newsletter to Jimmy Hemingway. In the eyes of the world Jimmy was "low man on the totem pole," someone to be hated, locked up and forgotten. But to the Body of Christ, He was a brother who was forgiven and loved, as are many of us.

Reaching Beyond

by Fred Little

I received the news about my Grandmother's passing while I was at work in the UVM Entomology Lab at the Northwest State Correctional Facility. It was 9:30 a.m. when the shift supervisor dropped by to deliver the news. I thanked him, shut down the lab and returned to the living unit to call home.

I spoke with my mother who informed me that Gram had gone into the hospital because she could not move her legs. Doctors had found a blood clot in one of her legs and performed emergency surgery to remove it. Unbeknownst to the medical staff, a piece of the blood clot had broken off during the operation and proceeded to travel toward Gram's brain. She died at 3:30 a.m. on February 20.

I told my Mom I would try to make the necessary arrangements to attend the funeral which was scheduled for the following week. Realizing that the Department of Corrections has no obligation to allow inmates to attend funerals, I offered the situation up to the Lord, letting Him know what the desire of my heart was, yet asking that His will be done.

My case worker and his supervisors were unavailable, so another case worker was assigned to assist in arranging a funeral transport. This person was also the liaison between UVM and NWSCF, so I had an established rapport with him. He called me into his office to tell me that he had been assigned to gather specific information pertaining to the funeral. This information, along with his recommendation, would be forwarded to the Superintendent to determine whether or not I would be allowed to attend.

After providing him with the details that he needed, I left his office and waited prayerfully for the official decision to come down.

Decisions on matters such as these usually are not rendered immediately, but only a few minutes had passed when my unit officer gave me a message to report back to the case worker's office. I was told that the arrangements had been made and that I would be attending the funeral on Monday afternoon! The case worker allowed me to call my family from the telephone in his office. Everyone was happy to hear that I would be able to attend, but no one more than me.

Over the weekend I thanked the Lord for arranging the funeral transport and asked Him to show me how I could glorify Him through this experience. By the time Monday arrived, I felt that the Lord may have given me a message. He had shown me in a dream that people would be speaking on Gram's behalf during her funeral, sharing their knowledge of her life and all of the trials she had encountered and conquered, and praising her for her strong character in the midst of turmoil. I felt that God was telling me that commending Gram's character was very respectful, but that He needed to receive the praise for her ability to endure the tremendous hardships she had faced.

I was concerned that some people attending the funeral would be intimidated or distracted by the fact that I would be there sporting shackles and hand cuffs. I asked the Lord to make the restraints invisible to those in attendance. Everyone's attention needed to be on Gram and each other, rather than on me.

I left NWSCF after lunch on Monday afternoon, sharing a transport van with another inmate who had violated conditions of release and was being delivered to the regional facility in South Burlington. He was very talkative and openly shared his frustration about having to be incarcerated again.

His addiction to marijuana had led him astray. He expressed great sorrow and concern for his girlfriend who, again, would be alone while he served more time. He said that he needed to settle down and get into contact with his "higher power." I saw this as an opportunity to witness to him, realizing that God wanted to use me to do his work. I shared some of my personal testimony and encouraged him to lean on Jesus Christ during this difficult time.

Upon our arrival at the South Burlington facility he thanked me for my counsel and gave me his mailing address. I promised to send him a tract explaining what it meant to be a follower of Jesus Christ, and a devotional booklet to help him establish a daily time with the Lord. God's presence was apparent as the van departed from South Burlington and proceeded on toward Huntington.

He was already at work.

It had been almost five years since I had last been to my hometown. It was a grey day, like a scene from an old black and white movie, as we traveled the winding mountain road toward home. Time seemed to disappear as a mixture of emotions and memories ran through my mind. Before I knew it we had reached our destination, the Huntington United Baptist Church.

A few of my family members were outside waiting for people to arrive, directing them to the church vestry where everyone was gathering. After greeting the people outside, my escorts and I joined the gathering in the vestry. I noticed my son standing near one of the windows that overlooked the river and immediately went over and gave him a hug and a kiss. He seemed to feel a little more comfortable being there now that his dad was present. The next few minutes were spent exchanging hugs and handshakes with relatives who I hadn't seen for several years. It seemed that every person there made it a point to greet me.

Next, the minister directed everyone to their appointed seats inside of the church. Once everybody was settled in, he began the service. This was a very personal service for the minister and the choir members because Gram had been a member of their congregation for most of her adult life. She had sung with the choir, helped with bake sales, and performed numerous other tasks. Curtains that she made still adorned the windows of the church vestry.

As the funeral progressed I thought about the dream, and in silent prayer asked the Lord for the opportunity to bear witness of Jesus Christ and to glorify His holy name. After sharing some of his personal reflections the minister called upon my step mother to share her prepared testimony about Gram's life. He also read the prepared testimony that my aunt had written.

Both of those testimonies described different aspects of Gram's life, emphasizing the hardships that she had faced raising five children in a single parent household during the forties and fifties. They spoke of the constant care and attention required of her to nurse one of my uncle's through a bout with polio and almost having to give up her children to foster care because of her financial status. Gram was credited for her tenacity and her ability to overcome difficulty. Reflecting back to the dream, I felt that the Lord had opened the door for me to point out the source of her strength.

When Reverend Martens finished reading my aunt's reflections, he asked if there was anyone else who would like to share a thought or memory of Gram with the congregation. As one of her friends shared his testimony, I prayed the Lord would provide the words I needed to bring His message forth. Again the opportunity to share a reflection was offered and I decided that it was my time to testify.

Speaking on behalf of my family, I thanked everyone for coming and sharing their memories of my grandmother with us. Confessing that I was not fully aware of all the hardships she had faced during her lifetime, I told them that the Lord had spoken to me and He wanted to let them know how Gram had conquered these adversities. I told them her faith in Jesus Christ and the promises of His gospel message had given her the ability to overcome life's challenges. I said I thought it would be very important to Gram that she not receive any credit for doing what she had done, that she wanted everyone there to understand that she could not have done it without the help of Jesus Christ, her Lord and Savior. I then challenged them to follow the example of Christ's likeness that Gram had set for us all, assuring everyone that her salvation was secure, and that theirs could be too. In conclusion, I read *Psalm 34*, in hopes that it would bring some comfort to their aching hearts.

Upon completion of the service, everyone moved back into the vestry for a brief reception. The message the Lord laid upon my heart had been received very well. Many people approached me tearfully and thanked me for sharing my testimony. I told them I appreciated their gratitude, but that they should be thanking God rather than me. After all, I was only a messenger.

The next half hour passed very quickly. Before I knew it, it was time for me to leave. I was grateful for the opportunity to attend the day's events, and to witness for the Lord, but my heart ached at the thought of having to leave everyone, especially my son. I said my goodbyes and gave everyone a departing hug, thanking them again for coming to show their respect for my grandmother. Then I was on my way.

The ride back to Saint Albans seemed to pass more slowly than the outgoing trip. I felt like a stranger passing through towns that I had lived in all of my life. As I reflected on the day that had come to pass, I realized that our God is a compassionate and loving God. He had granted me the desire of my heart by allowing me to attend my grandmother's funeral and He cared enough about my family and friends to send them an eternal message. Acknowledging God's presence helped me to put my emotions into perspective, adding a glimmer of light to the darkness of the day.

Upon returning to NWSCF, I had dinner and then phoned my Dad. I wanted to check on him, and everyone else, to see how they were doing. During our conversation he told me that a friend of the family who attended the funeral was inquiring about me, asking him how long I had been out of jail. Dad informed him that I was still incarcerated and that I had been transported to the church by two prison guards, asking him, "Didn't you see the handcuffs and shackles that Fred was wearing?" His answer was, "No, I didn't. Nor did I see the two prison guards." Even more incredible was the fact that his wife had prompted him to inquire about me! Apparently she didn't see the guards or constraints either!

God had made them invisible!

Phyllis Russell

The Church at Prison conference this year was attended by about 50 people from around Vermont with our keynote speakers, Johnny & Betty Moffit coming from Texas. One of the highlights of the conference was Agnes Fiske presenting a letter to Jenni Chamberlin, daughter of the late Phyllis Russell, that announced the formation of the Phyllis Russell Memorial Fund. Here is the text of that letter:

To: The Family of Phyllis Russell:

Phyllis Russell was an inspiration to those of us who work in prison ministry in Vermont. She was dedicated to presenting the Gospel of Jesus Christ to prisoners for twenty-two years. She touched the lives of thousands of men and women in Vermont Prisons. Only God will ever know the full impact of her work for Him.

On May 5, 2000 at The Church At Prison Conference we are announcing the formation of The Phyllis Russell Memorial Fund. The fund will be used to provide Vermont prisoners with opportunities for Continuing Christian Education. Phyllis' home church, Maranatha Christian Church, has seeded the fund with its first donation pledge.

The Fund will be managed by The Church At Prison Inc. with candidates being reviewed for approval by The Church at Prison Board of Directors or their designee. Recommendations of applicants will be received through Prison Ministries and Ministers with whom we network in Vermont.

As God is moving and changing the lives of men and women incarcerated in Vermont Prisons it is becoming apparent to many of us that the best prison ministers are the indigenous ministers that God is raising up within the prison population. Rather than wait for their release to provide Bible College Education, we are being moved by God to provide training, education, and opportunities for Ministry while they are incarcerated.

Through The Church at Prison, Patmos Christian College, and The Phyllis Russell Memorial Fund it will be possible for approved Vermont prisoners to receive training, education, and ministry assignments leading to licensing and ordination, specifically for Prison Ministry, while still in prison. It is hoped that many of these individuals will, after release, continue their work in Prison Ministry.

God Bless you!

Pastor Pete Fiske

VII.

VERMONT DEPT. OF CORRECTIONS

CSOM
(Center for Sex Offender Management)

In February, 1998 the US Department of Justice sent Agnes and me to Phoenix, Arizona to attend a conference sponsored by The Center for Sex Offender Management (CSOM). Just before this we attended our son Lee's wedding in Santo Domingo, Dominican Republic. He had traveled to Santo Domingo, met Magalys Jacqueline Ruis Sierra, a Christian woman introduced to him by Aqsa Johnson, daughter of Bishop William Johnson. Aqsa had met her while attending medical school in Santo Domingo. Lee had traveled to Pakistan on three missionary journeys to work with William. At the time of the wedding, Lee was also pastoring an English speaking church service on Sunday afternoons with mostly medical students from Nigeria.

Lee's wedding was on Friday, February 20th and the next day we were on the plane to Phoenix. The purpose of the meeting was to bring together teams from ten US Corrections locations that have innovative methods in managing sex offenders being released from prisons. By sharing various methods being used, setting goals for the teams to further develop their methods, and providing Federal Funding for projects, the team intended to improve the management of sex offenders nationwide.

The Vermont team consisted of Bob McGrath & Georgia Cumming from the Vermont Treatment Program for Sexual Aggressors (VTPSA), Dianne Smith from Probation & Parole, Sister Lorraine Ambrozini, a Department of Corrections (DOC) Volunteer, and myself and Agnes, representing the Church At Prison. Vermont was chosen because of our involvement in supporting high-risk sexual offenders being released with "intensive support teams." We also brought Evan Heisy from the Mennonite Central Office in Toronto, Canada to train our teams with their methods of Circles of Support and Accountability (COSA). Vermont DOC took advantage of this training and eventually were able to establish COSA teams in Vermont.

This is a Ministry direction that we never expected.

I was sent to another CSOM Conference in Baltimore, Maryland from December 7-9 1998, as part of the Vermont Team. These gatherings continued in Boston, Massachusetts and Portland, Oregon with the intent of improving the management and supervision of released sex offenders nationwide. Vermont DOC received funding for VTPSA projects through CSOM.

CSOM eventually developed a website that provided literature on the best practices and clinical information on supervision of sex offenders. This project is now part of Center for Effective Public Policy:
https://cepp.com/project/center-for-sex-offender-management-csom/

The Church At Prison pioneered methods that opened pathways for others to follow and perfect.

Relations With Vermont Dept. of Corrections RE: Wayne Delisle

God has blessed us with excellent working relations with the Vermont Department of Corrections (DOC). Our support team recruitment and training has been recognized as a very valuable asset to DOC and offenders being released.

Another way God blessed us was involvement in a difficult offender release case. In 1995, after his murder conviction was overturned, Wayne Delisle was released on probation in Vermont. The media broadcast his release in sensationalized ways that created panic, resulting in the worst public protest Vermont DOC had ever experienced. The media continuously published the locations where Wayne was placed by DOC, and neighbors would show up to protest. A violent offender, notorious and ruthless in northern Vermont, Wayne had become a modern day Frankenstein, the mob of outraged townspeople coming to drive him out with torches and pitch forks.

After being turned down by three other states for permission to transfer, the offender came to The Church at Prison (CAP) for safekeeping until a state could be found that would accept him.

We were able to set up a series of safe homes for Wayne to stay that kept him out of view of the public and media. Eventually, through a network of ministry contacts, we found a Christian businessman in another state who would provide him with a job and apartment. Vermont DOC worked with that state and transferred him to their probation department.

This project brought us the sincere gratitude of DOC Commissioner John Gorczyk and his staff (see letters of commendation from John Gorczyk and Gail LeBlanc).

VT DOC works with us to train volunteers we recruit by participating in our Conferences as speakers and workshop leaders. We, in turn, speak at their seminars and trainings. We have also participated in some of their treatment program sessions. Through VT DOC we have worked with NIC (the National Institute of Corrections) and CSOM (The Center for Management of Sex Offenders). Both are agencies with the US Justice Department.

Relocating 1:
Wayne Delisle

Occasionally an inmate considered to be dangerous and who was also high profile in the media would be released, and we were asked to relocate him. Wayne Delisle was the first such inmate we worked with. He had been convicted of murder, but his case was overturned. Rather than go through another trial, seven years after the conviction, the prosecutor decided to place him on lifetime probation. His release was highly publicized and the media labeled him as a dangerous murderer. Wherever Vermont DOC located him, the media alongside a mob of citizens would find out and harass him. Finally, Vermont DOC had no other option but to transfer him to New York where he would live with his daughter. As usual, the media found out and created a circus. The daughter's husband lost his job over it, she and her husband were asked to leave the trailer park where they lived, and Governor Pataki told Wayne he had to leave the state of New York.

When Vermont DOC asked me to try to relocate Wayne, I met him secretly in Rutland and took him under cover to our home in St. Albans. The news media in Vermont was looking for him intently. Wayne was big news and the media was sensationalizing his case to scare people and boost ratings. So Wayne maintained a low profile, had a hat pulled down over his face whenever he left the house, and used hair coloring to get rid of the gray. I was notified by Vermont DOC Central Office that we should move him to a different location every night. DOC was required to notify law enforcement or community officials whenever he stayed overnight in their community.

For the most part Wayne stayed in the homes of pastors who knew him and worked with our ministry. One night, for lack of a place to stay, Wayne was put in a homeless shelter in Barre. The police were notified and immediately the media found out. This resulted in an angry mob of citizens heading to the shelter to drive him out. Wayne didn't wait. He went out the back door and hid in a nearby graveyard, where I picked him up and transferred him to a pastor's home in Montpelier. The prospect of being attacked by an angry mob, and hiding amongst graves at midnight hoping that I would show up to rescue him was a bit much for Wayne. But God was good and kept him safe and sane until I got there.

A few days later Wayne and I were sitting in a state office waiting room. He had a cap pulled down to cover his face, trying to look inconspicuous. He happened to look at his prison issue shoes with white toes and realized that on the toes was written in bold letters "Wayne Delisle." We hoped nobody saw that because his name was all over the news headlines: "Where is Wayne Delisle"?

Eventually, I was able to make arrangements with a Christian in another state who provided a room and a job to get Wayne started.

Relocating 2:
Tim Szad

In 1999 a tall man came into the North West Church Service and introduced himself: "I'm Tim Szad." I looked up, but had to look up higher to see his face. He was six feet, six inches tall. After meeting with him for pastoral counseling a couple times, he accepted the Lord Jesus and wanted to be baptized. With warm weather comes the opportunity to use a portable tank for baptisms. He was so tall I joked, "We might have to break your legs to get you in there." But he was able to fit and was baptized.

Years later he came to the end of his sentence, and the media had a field day sensationalizing his pending release.

The original plan for his release was to live with his parents in Springfield, but because of the media attention (local, national and international) his parents received all sort of threats. At the very last moment, Vermont DOC called us for help in relocating him out of state. It seemed impossible with his notoriety, but God opened a way to San Francisco with help from a former client who had previously been relocated.

At 4:00 a.m. on the day of his release, before the media arrived to sensationalize the event, Tim was escorted to the private car of the Chief of Security, Joshua Rutherford. Tim was asked to lay down in the back seat so he would not be seen, in case the media had arrived. Joshua drove Tim to Bradley Airport in Connecticut, gave him $600 cash, and wished him well.

After 13 years of incarceration, unharassed by the media or news, Tim boarded a plane bound for San Francisco as a free man. It seemed a monumental success.

Arriving in San Francisco, Tim located the room he would be staying in with the help of a previous client who we had also relocated to the city. Tim registered his presence with the police, who knew he was coming. When they asked him, "How long will you be staying?" he didn't know what to say. The next morning there was a police cruiser parked in front of Tim's residence. At least twice a day a policeman would knock on the door and ask, "Are you leaving today?"

After a few days Tim began to feel aggravated and unwelcomed, then decided to leave San Francisco in hopes of finding a more peaceful place to settle down. He took a bus north. At the next stop he hoped to find a more friendly community, but the local police were waiting for him and convinced him to continue north. I told Tim we had a connection in Portland, Oregon who could offer some advice there.

When he arrived in Portland he stayed overnight at Motel 6. Apparently, the police in Portland were expecting him and saw him get off the bus, but did not know he was at Motel 6. The next morning he went to the Portland police station to check in with the registry officer. She handed him a bus ticket and told him she was sending him back to Burlington, VT and Pastor Pete. She looked at him without blinking and said, "Get on that bus or I will shoot you."

This is not what Tim had expected for his newfound freedom after serving his entire sentence and being released from prison as a free man and legal citizen.

After boarding the bus Tim called me and told me he was on the way back to Vermont. I was his only support contact and had 5 days to figure out how to handle the situation. The media would be waiting in Burlington for him at the bus station—which would be disastrous for Tim and whatever plans we had to house him. To avoid this I recruited another volunteer, Steve Brown, to travel with me to White River Junction, located almost 100 miles southeast of Burlington, on the New Hampshire border, where we intercepted Tim at the bus station in this smaller town. There, we located a client in a motel who allowed Tim to take a shower, change into clean clothes, and grab a bite to eat before we hit the road.

We drove to Burlington and met with the Chief of Police Mike Stirling and an officer from the Chittenden Unit for Special Investigations. They welcomed Tim and offered their assistance to help him integrate back into society in Vermont.

I got a room for Tim at a Motel 6 and stayed the night as his chaperon. Eventually, we found a Christian home in Hyde Park that was willing to provide a room for Tim.

The next day Tim and I met with Lamoille County Sheriff Roger Marcoux in his Hyde Park office. Sheriff Marcoux introduced himself by saying that his job was to protect the citizens of Lamoille County and now Tim was one of those citizens. After the meeting there was an interview with WCAX TV News in the parking lot. Both Sheriff Marcoux and I spoke. We set the record straight and they reported the truth about Tim instead of fearmongering and scaring the public.

A productive relationship between Tim and Sheriff Marcoux developed, and Tim became a carpenter on staff with the Sheriff's Dept. Tim is a master carpenter and helped construct a service building for the department vehicles, with a second story storage armory for confiscated weapons.

The relationship between Tim and the Sheriff's Dept. became newsworthy and was reported in two articles by Seven Days newspaper. Through providing the support that is guided by God, we were able to transform Tim's story of tragedy into one of redemption and hope. Tim now also crafts wooden crosses for the Church at Prison, an expression of his gratitude and belief in the loving salvation of God.

Letters of Acknowledgement and Gratitude from VT Dept of Corrections

Agency of Human Services
DEPARTMENT OF CORRECTIONS
103 South Main Street
Waterbury, VT 05671-1001

August 7, 1995

Mr. Pete Fiske
P. O. Box 1128
St. Albans, VT. 05478

Dear Mr. Fiske,

DOC staff in Burlington have advised that you were of tremendous help in working with Wayne Delisle. I want to express my thanks, as well.

It is so important to recognize, as you do, that working with offenders is a team effort requiring the cooperation of community members and Department personnel. We are fortunate to have working with us volunteers such as yourself who combine compassion with an ability to respond to a crisis so that they can really get things done. Your initiative and follow-through in getting Mr. Delisle situated are examples of this.

My thanks, as well, extend to all those who worked with you and I would appreciate it if you would relay that to them all.

Please accept my appreciation for all the volunteer work that you have done on behalf of DOC clients and staff during the last several years, as well as this most recent situation. We look forward to continued work with you.

Sincerely.

John F. Gorczyk
Commissioner

AGENCY OF HUMAN SERVICES
DEPARTMENT OF CORRECTIONS
PROBATION & PAROLE
50 Cherry St.
BURLINGTON, VERMONT 05401
PHONE: (802) 863-7350

August 4, 1995

Mr. Pete Fiske
P. O. Box 1128
St. Albans, VT. 05478

Dear Pete,

It is difficult to express adequately the appreciation we feel for all that you have done to help ease the situation with Wayne Delisle during these past couple of weeks. To say that "we couldn't have done it without you" is an understatement. your cooperative spirit, your compassion, your persistence, as well as your ability to organize others has been extraordinary. It has truly been a privilege to work with you.

Please pass along our appreciation as well to all those who worked with you during this crisis and let them know that they have our gratitude and respect.

I look forward to working with you on future, hopefully less dramatic, projects.

Sincerely

Gail LeBlanc, Superintendent
Burlington Community Corrections Service Center

VERMONT CENTER FOR PREVENTION
AND TREATMENT OF SEXUAL ABUSE
50 Cherry St., Burlington, VT 05401

October 22, 1997

To Whom it May Concern:

I write this letter to support the expansion of the ministry of Pastor Pete and Agnes Fiske and The Church at Prison.

I have known Pastor Pete and Agnes Fiske for approximately two years in my role as Clinical Director of the Vermont Treatment Program for Sexual Aggressors (VTPSA). The VTPSA is the Vermont Department of Corrections' network of prison and community based sex offender treatment programs.

The work of this ministry has been an extremely important component in the success of our sex offender treatment programs. When sex offenders are released from prison they need community support systems to assist them with what is often a difficult adjustment. Unfortunately, sex offenders have often been rejected by their family and friends because of the nature of their crimes. For this reason, it is so important for these men to have someone who cares about them and also helps hold them accountable for managing their risk in the community. The ministry has been very successful in finding and training volunteers to help several of the men who have graduated from our incarcerated sex offender programs. However, volunteers need ongoing training and supervision to provides this type of service and I know that the resources of the ministry are often stretched.

I also want to note that I have observed the ministry having an important influence beyond Vermont. For example, Pastor Pete spoke to a group of mental health and corrections professionals at a national seminar held in Burlington this spring sponsored by the U.S. Department of Justice. Seminar participants from several states were very impressed with the Church's efforts and began to see how they might work with clergy in their own states to better help offenders and prevent victimization.

The ministry models a way of working with the men in our program that inspires a wonderful blend of spirit, pragmatism, hope, and respect. I support any effort that can help the ministry continue and expand this important work.

Please feel free to contact me if you need any further information.

Sincerely,

Robert J. McGrath, M. A.
Clinical Director
Vermont Treatment Program for Sexual Aggressors

VERMONT CENTER FOR PREVENTION
AND TREATMENT OF SEXUAL ABUSE
50 Cherry Street, Burlington, VT 05401
Telephone: 802-651-1661
September 29, 1997

To Whom It May Concern:

I am writing to speak about my experience working with The Church at Prison Ministry and thereby lend my support to their grant application.

    I am the Program Coordinator for the Vermont Treatment Program for Sexual Aggressors (VTPSA). An important aspect of our treatment program is the transition from the incarcerated program to living in the community under parole or furlough supervision. Many of our offenders have little or no family and/or community support under upon their release. Pastor Pete and Agnes have been instrumental in developing support teams for those offenders who need this help. With Pete finding volunteers around the state interested in doing this invaluable but stressful work, I, and other Correctional Staff provide the specialized training. After training, the identified team will meet with the offender and our staff and begin the important work of offense disclosure, review of risk factors and what the team and the offender's responsibility will be once that offender is in the community.

    I cannot stress enough the importance of the relationship between volunteer and offender. The sex offender is often ostracized by the community who may not understand the dynamics of sexual abuse or may not believe sex offenders can change their sexually abusive behavior. Sex offenders often isolate themselves because of their shame and guilt and think they are not worthy of friendships. Volunteers provide an important link for the sex offender reintegrating back into the community safely.

    Before The Church at Prison Ministry began to work with our program, I had worked with the Department of Corrections' Volunteer Coordinators in finding volunteers to work with our clients. We were successful in only one county. Pete's contacts are throughout the state. When I need a support team in a county I contact Pete and he finds volunteers. In one county we even have a monthly support group for volunteers working with sex offenders.

Pete also provides an important link between volunteers and our Department. My favorite training with volunteers is to have Pete present so he can model the supportive but highly accountable relationship that should have with sex offenders. My job would be much more difficult without the assistance and support that Pete provides. If there is further information you require, please call me al 802-651-1661.

Sincerely,

Georgia Cumming
Program Coordinator, VTPSA

STATE OF VERMONT
AGENCY OF HUMAN SERVICES
NORTHWEST STATE CORRECTIONAL FACILITY
R.F.D. #1, BOX 279-1, SWANTON, VT 05488
TELEPHONE: (802) 524-6771

September 3, 1997

Pastor Pete Fiske
Church of the Northwest
RFD #1, Box 279-1
Swanton, VT 05488

To Whom It May Concern;

Over the past several years Pete and Agnes Fiske have been volunteering here at the Northwest State Correctional Facility. Out of their work here came the Church of the Northwest: a ministry with a healthy following of offenders who have found religion and spirituality to be a necessary part of beginning a new way of life. The Church, and the Fiske's themselves, are seen as a very valuable asset to the facility.

Having worked with the Department for some 17 years, I can say that I have never seen volunteers, religious or otherwise, have a more collaborative relationship with Department staff. The Fiske's and their ministry are often called upon to help in crisis. They have done spiritual counseling, marriage counseling and crisis intervention with offenders that are depressed, distraught or even suicidal. Most recently, the facility had to deal with a whole new issue: offenders transitioning to the street directly without stepping out through a regional facility (Policy Change). The Fiske's were right there to help, they saw a need and offered to get involved by helping offenders find good, healthy, spiritual, support people that would be willing to help them once released on furlough.

Both staff and offenders regularly turn to the Fiske's and their ministry to help deal with issues or problems that arise in the facility. They are trusted, respected and supported by all. As a member of the facility administration, I count myself lucky to have volunteers like the Fiske's . They have the willingness and ability to offer guidance in many areas both spiritual and otherwise. They are special.

Sincerely,

Brian M. Bilodeau
Assistant Superintendent
Northwest State Correctional Facility

Afterword

Thank you for reading this book. My purpose is to encourage you to follow God's calling in your life, in faith, knowing that he will supply all of your needs.

I knew nothing, but God knew everything. I was lost, but God gave me direction. I was poor, but God owns everything and shared his bounty. I was scared, but God demanded courage. I was surrounded by enemies, but God prepared a table before me in their presence. I didn't know how to react, but God shared His wisdom. I didn't know what to say, but God put words in my mouth.

When I was 20 and lonely, God brought Agnes Dutelle into my life to be my wife and ministry partner. At 60, after 39 years of marriage, my first wife had died and I was alone again. At 62 God brought Joanne Falise into my life as my new wife and ministry partner.

God has been good to me.

The greatest thing a human can experience is to know God and fulfill His purpose for their life. He is the greatest boss I ever had. As I approach my time to be with Him, I reflect more on His goodness in my life!

About the Author

Pastor Pete Fiske a 6th generation Vermonter who resides in Jericho, Vermont with his wife Pastor Joanne Reed Fiske, their Border Collie "Asher" and Maine Coon Cat "Simba". They enjoy hiking the pine forest trails that surround their home, where Pete is also an avid trail camera buff. He is the founder of The Church At Prison, Inc. and has 5 sons, 12 grandchildren and 14 great grandchildren. Inspired by God, Pete wrote this book to encourage people to follow the calling God has on their lives.

He can be reached by email at pastorpete@churchatprison.com and via his website at https://dontburnmyhousedown.org

Made in the USA
Columbia, SC
28 March 2025